Don't Leave Me Here

Also by Maggie Hartley

Tiny Prisoners
Too Scared to Cry
The Little Ghost Girl
A Family for Christmas
Too Young to be a Mum
Who Will Love Me Now?
The Girl No One Wanted
Battered, Broken, Healed
Is it My Fault, Mummy?
Sold to be a Wife
Denied a Mummy
A Desperate Cry for Help
Daddy's Little Soldier
Please, Don't Take My Sisters
Not to Blame
Exploited
Groomed to be a Bride
The Lost Boy
A Sister's Shame
Behind Closed Doors
Please Give My Baby Back
Where's My Mummy?
Nobody Loves Me
Please Don't Take Mummy Away
Will You Help Me?
A Sister for Christmas
Please Help My Mummy

Don't Leave Me Here

SASKIA'S TRUE STORY OF SECRETS,
KIDNAP AND ABUSE

MAGGIE HARTLEY

WITH
HEATHER BISHOP

SEVEN DIALS

First published in Great Britain in 2025 by Seven Dials,
an imprint of The Orion Publishing Group Ltd
Carmelite House, 50 Victoria Embankment
London EC4Y 0DZ

An Hachette UK Company

The authorised representative in the EEA is Hachette Ireland,
8 Castlecourt Centre, Dublin 15, D15 XTP3, Ireland
(email: info@hbgi.ie)

1 3 5 7 9 10 8 6 4 2

Copyright © Maggie Hartley Limited 2025

The moral right of Maggie Hartley to be identified as
the author of this work has been asserted in accordance
with the Copyright, Designs and Patents Act of 1988.

All rights reserved. No part of this publication may be
reproduced, stored in a retrieval system, or transmitted
in any form or by any means, electronic, mechanical,
photocopying, recording, or otherwise, without the
prior permission of both the copyright owner and the
above publisher of this book.

A CIP catalogue record for this book is
available from the British Library.

**Please be aware that this book includes discussions of a
range of sensitive subjects, including abuse.**

ISBN (Mass Market Paperback) 978 1 3996 2925 6
ISBN (Ebook) 978 1 3996 2926 3
ISBN (Audio) 978 1 3996 2927 0

Typeset by Born Group
Printed and bound in Great Britain by Clays Ltd, Elcograf S.p.A.

www.orionbooks.co.uk

Dedication

This book is dedicated to Saskia, PJ and all the children who have passed through my home. It's been a privilege to have cared for you and to be able to share your stories. And to the children who live with me now – thank you for your determination, strength and joy, and for sharing your lives with me.

Contents

	A Message from Maggie	ix
ONE	A Lost Cause	1
TWO	Peace and Quiet	13
THREE	Introductions	25
FOUR	A Reunion	35
FIVE	Compare and Contrast	49
SIX	Turnaround	59
SEVEN	Conflict	71
EIGHT	Secrets and Lies	83
NINE	An Unwelcome Visitor	95
TEN	Caught in the Act	105
ELEVEN	Questions Not Answers	115
TWELVE	Coming Clean	123

THIRTEEN	*Secrecy and Shock*	135
FOURTEEN	*The Unknown*	149
FIFTEEN	*Aftermath*	159
SIXTEEN	*Searching for Answers*	171
SEVENTEEN	*A Waiting Game*	183
EIGHTEEN	*Justice*	197
NINETEEN	*Courage and Cowards*	207
TWENTY	*Flying Free*	219
	Acknowledgements	231

A Message from Maggie

I wanted to write this book to give people an honest account of what it's like to be a foster carer, to talk about some of the challenges that I face on a day-to-day basis and about some of the children that I've helped.

My main concern throughout all this is to protect the children who have been in my care. For this reason, all names and identifying details have been changed, including my own, and no locations have been included.

Being a foster carer is a privilege and I couldn't imagine doing anything else. My house is never quiet but I wouldn't have it any other way. I hope perhaps my stories will inspire other people to consider fostering as new carers are always desperately needed. In fact, there's currently a recruitment crisis facing the foster community – across the UK, there's currently a shortage of 6,500 foster families.[*] It comes at the same time as the number of children in care in the UK is expected to rise to 95,000 in 2025.[†] Foster carers are needed more than ever, so please do look into it if it's something that you or someone you know has ever considered.

---

[*] The Fostering Network. 'More children to end up in unsuitable homes if more foster carers aren't urgently recruited', 13 May 2024. Available at: https://www.thefosteringnetwork.org.uk/news/more-children-to-end-up-in-unsuitable-homes-if-more-foster-carers-aren-t-urgently-recruited/ (accessed 16 April 2025).

[†] County Councils Network. 'Number of children in care could reach almost 100,000 by 2025 – as county leaders call for an "unrelenting" focus on keeping families together', 22 November 2021. Available at: https://www.countycouncilsnetwork.org.uk/number-of-children-in-care-could-reach-almost-100000-by-2025-as-county-leaders-call-for-an-unrelenting-focus-on-keeping-families-together/ (accessed 16 April 2025).

ONE

A Lost Cause

Thud.

Suddenly, my eyes flicked open and I sat up in bed.

What was that?

It was 11.30 p.m. and I'd only been in bed for half an hour. But sitting there in the darkness, the only thing I could hear was the sound of the blood rushing in my ears.

I must have been imagining it.

I lay back down and rested my head on the pillow. For the past week, I'd been living on adrenalin and seemed to be in a constant state of high alert.

I was currently fostering thirteen-year-old PJ. He was the only placement that I had at the moment, but he was a challenge to say the least.

He'd been in the care system since he was eleven, after his mum had left the area, abandoning him. Neighbours had found him starving and alone in his flat three days later, living off crisps and sweets he'd stolen from the local shop.

Over the past two years his behaviour had got worse as he was moved from one carer to another. Sadly, it was something I was seeing more and more frequently. He'd come to me after his current foster carers said they could no longer cope.

Never one to shy away from tricky placements, I'd said I'd take him in temporarily while a long-term solution was found.

For the first week or so, PJ had been fine. I wouldn't have called him chatty, but he had been OK, and he went to school and came straight home. Although he'd spent most of the time in his bedroom, we'd managed to have dinner together. I thought his previous foster carers must have been exaggerating about his behaviour. It was a few days later that I realised he had lulled me into a false sense of security. Things changed dramatically.

PJ had been skipping school and not coming home until late in the evening. When he did come back, he stank of weed. I'd noticed money had gone missing from my purse, so I'd started keeping my handbag locked away in my bedroom and updated his social worker and my supervising social worker about my suspicions.

This evening, he'd not come back after school until 10 p.m. – much too late for a thirteen-year-old.

'I won't tolerate this kind of behaviour in my house,' I'd told PJ when he'd finally turned up. 'As a foster carer, it's my responsibility to know where you are. So I need you to come straight home from school tomorrow. Do you understand?'

He'd shrugged, with his head down, and had spent the rest of the evening in his bedroom.

Before I'd gone to bed, I'd knocked on his door.

'What?' he'd grunted.

I'd pushed it open a chink.

'Night, PJ. Remember what I said about coming straight home tomorrow.'

'Yep,' he'd muttered.

It was a relief to see that he was already in his pyjamas and curled up in bed.

He was probably fast asleep by now and, if I could stop my mind playing tricks on me, I knew I needed to do the same.

I closed my eyes and tried to relax but I was still on hyper alert, listening out for any sound.

It's OK, I told myself. *You're imagining things.*

But sadly I wasn't.

Thud.

This time, there was no mistaking it. I jumped up out of bed and grabbed my dressing gown. PJ's bedroom door was closed but I could see the glow of a light coming from underneath it.

'PJ?' I asked, knocking on the door. 'Are you OK?'

No answer.

'I just want to check that you're OK in there.'

Silence.

'I'm coming in, I need to make sure you're OK.' I pushed open the door to find an empty bed and no sign of PJ.

'Oh no,' I gasped.

I bolted downstairs, as I realised that was where the noise must have been coming from. I ran into the kitchen first. I'd double-locked the front door and the patio doors and had put the keys in the kitchen drawer. Thankfully, they were still there. Then I dashed into the living room at the front of the house. Naively, I thought maybe he was in there watching TV.

But as I pushed open the door, a cold breeze hit me and told me everything I needed to know.

The lock on one of the bottom sash windows had been unscrewed. It was wide open, and PJ was gone. My bedroom was directly above the living room and I realised that the thud I'd heard must have been him opening the window.

With my heart racing, I unlocked the front door and ran out into the street. But it was too late. Even in the glow of the streetlights, I could see there was no sign of PJ. He had disappeared into the darkness.

It was always horrendous when a child went missing on your watch, particularly when it was a child you'd only been caring for for a few days.

I'd done it enough times over the years to know the drill by now.

First, I called the out-of-hours number at my agency and let them know that PJ had run off.

'I'll let Social Services know,' said Marion, the social worker on duty. 'If you could call the police, Maggie, and report him as missing and then ring me back with the crime number, that would be helpful.'

'Will do,' I said.

I knew the only issue with calling the police at this time of night was that they always took hours to come. A troubled thirteen-year-old who was in care sadly wasn't going to be at the top of the list of their priorities, especially one who had gone AWOL before. Once I'd reported PJ missing and got back to Social Services, I made myself a cup of tea to calm my nerves and settled onto the sofa.

I was shattered but I knew there was no point going back to bed, as there was a chance I wouldn't hear the door when the police arrived or if PJ came back. Besides, I was too worried and on edge to sleep. Over the years, I'd had several teenagers who had gone missing from time to time – in fact, there was one boy who ran off every couple of days. It was always concerning and stressful, but I knew all I could do was go through the proper processes and thankfully the police would always bring them back – or they'd eventually come back of their own accord. It was never a nice experience to go through, though.

It wasn't the most comfortable sofa, but it had acted as a makeshift bed for me many times over the years. As I tossed and turned, all I could think about was PJ. He thought he was tough and streetwise – but he was only thirteen and I knew that inside he was just a scared, vulnerable little boy who had been abandoned by his mother. My mind couldn't stop ticking over and over. *Where was he? Who was he with? What was he doing?*

I didn't sleep a wink and, just after 1 a.m., there was finally a knock at the door. I jumped up to answer it. Two female officers were standing on the doorstep. They held up their IDs and I showed them in.

'I'm PC Penny Brent and this is PC Helen Biller,' one of them said.

'I'm assuming that you need to search the house first?' I asked them.

They both nodded apologetically.

'You must have gone through this before?' asked PC Brent.

'Sadly, many times over the years with a variety of children,' I replied.

There was a protocol they had to follow when a child went missing and the first step was a thorough search of the house they had been in, just to check they weren't hiding somewhere. I knew of one foster carer who'd reported a child missing and it turned out they were hiding under their bed the whole time, so it could happen.

I'd done a quick check in every room myself and I was sure that PJ wasn't in the house, but I knew the officers had to check. I waited downstairs while they opened every cupboard, checked under every bed and even searched the shed in my back garden. I was relieved that I wasn't fostering any other children, otherwise they would have been disturbed by the search too.

As I'd expected, PJ was nowhere to be seen. Afterwards, I made us all a cup of tea while the officers took a statement from me.

'Has PJ done this before?' asked PC Biller.

'Not with me,' I said. 'He's been hours late after school but he's not gone missing this late before.'

'Do you have the names of any of his friends or know where he likes to hang out?' she added.

'Unfortunately, I don't know that much about him, as he's only just come to live with me.' I wrung my hands.

'You look worried,' said PC Brent.

'I *am* worried,' I replied. 'It's the middle of the night and he's only thirteen. He's missing and there's no guarantee that he's safe. People could be taking advantage of him. It's terrifying.'

'I can understand,' PC Brent nodded. 'We'll circulate his description to all of the local units and we'll do a drive round the local area and the town centre. Hopefully we'll have him back to you soon.'

'I hope so,' I said.

It was after 2 a.m. by the time the police left. I knew it was pointless trying to sleep now as I was wide awake and wanted to make sure that I heard PJ if he came back, as he didn't have a key. I decided to sit on the sofa and watch a film, desperately hoping I'd be disturbed by a tap on the window or a knock on the door.

By the time the film ended, there was still no sign of him. At some point during the second film, my eyes must have closed and I nodded off.

When I came round, daylight was streaming in through the living-room window. I looked at my watch. It was 8 a.m. and I could hear the hustle and bustle of the street outside as people headed off to work and school.

Maybe PJ was back and I hadn't woken up? I knew it was unlikely but I told myself perhaps he'd stolen a key and taken it with him, or forced his way in somehow? I rushed upstairs but my heart sank when I saw his empty bed.

It was at times like these that I was thankful I had no other children living with me at the time; I'd had a couple of respite placements that had lasted for a few months before PJ, as well as two longer-term placements. There was Amena, who I'd fostered for more than a year while her mum was in France caring for her aunt who was sadly dying of cancer. Then baby Felix, who I'd fostered for six months until he was able to be returned to live with his mum, Emily. Feeling like this, it would have been hard having to get up early and look after a baby or toddler, or even get another child to school.

I had a quick shower and got dressed but I was too tired and anxious to eat any breakfast. When it got to 9 a.m., I phoned my supervising social worker Becky as I knew she'd be starting work.

'Maggie, I've just read the update from the out-of-hours social worker,' she told me. 'Has PJ turned up yet?'

'No,' I sighed. 'Still no sign.'

'I'll give his social worker Carrie a ring and see if his former carers can think of anywhere he might have gone or who he might be with,' she told me.

'Good idea,' I agreed. 'It would be good to give the police that information.'

I also rang PJ's school and told them that he'd gone missing and wouldn't be coming in that day.

'Not for the first time,' sighed the receptionist.

By midday, nothing had changed. I hadn't heard anything from the police so I knew there couldn't be any update. To take my mind off things, I vacuumed the bedrooms, mopped the bathroom floor and dusted and tidied up everywhere. Cleaning was always my therapy when I was feeling stressed or anxious.

I was lugging the vacuum cleaner down the stairs when I heard a noise.

I stopped in my tracks as I heard a quiet knock on the front door.

Holding my breath, I opened it to find a dishevelled-looking PJ standing there.

'Thank goodness,' I sighed. 'I've been so worried about you. Where have you been?'

'Nowhere,' he scowled, pushing past me. He ran up the stairs and I heard his bedroom door slam.

I decided to let him cool off a bit before I tried to talk to him.

I called Becky first.

'He's just walked in,' I told her.

'What a relief!' she said. 'Where's he been?'

'Absolutely no idea,' I replied. 'He wouldn't talk to me.'

I told her what had happened and that he'd gone straight to his bedroom.

'I'll try to have a chat to him in a bit,' I said.

After I'd put the phone down, I called the police. PC Brent had given me her mobile number.

'PJ's just got back,' I told her.

'Oh, that is good news,' she replied. 'We'll come round.'

When a missing child returned, the police had to see them for themselves and talk with them about why they'd disappeared.

'We're going off shift soon so we'll head back round to you now,' she said.

'OK,' I nodded.

Two police officers turning up to talk to PJ might be exactly what he needed to realise that he couldn't behave like this.

Ten minutes later, I was just about to go up and check in with PJ as I knew the officers would be here soon, when suddenly he appeared in the kitchen doorway.

'You must be starving,' I said to him. 'Shall I make you something to eat?'

He looked at me and scowled.

'Who was you talking to?' he grunted. 'I heard you on the phone.'

'I was telling Social Services that you were back,' I told him. 'We were all really worried about you. The police were out looking for you too.'

I paused.

'They're going to come round now and have a chat with you about where you've been.'

'The police?' he shouted. 'Why the f*** did you call them? I don't wanna talk to the f***ing police!'

'PJ, you can't just go missing like that,' I told him. 'You're only thirteen.'

'I'll do what the f*** I want! I ain't taking orders from you!'

Suddenly there was a knock at the door and PJ froze.

'That will be the police now,' I told him. 'They just want to make sure you're safe.'

'I told you, I don't wanna talk to them,' he snarled. He glanced up at me. There was a rage in his eyes that made my blood run cold.

I tried to brush past him to let them in but as I did, he grabbed my arm. Even though he was only thirteen, he was already taller than me and his grip was strong.

'Don't answer the door,' he hissed.

Before I knew what was happening, he pushed me to the floor. Then he lifted one of the kitchen dining chairs up in the air.

'PJ, no!' I shouted, instinctively holding my arms up to protect my face.

But it was too late. He threw the wooden chair and it hit me directly on the head.

My body trembled in shock and my head throbbed. I blinked as I felt something dripping into my right eye. As I raised my hand up to it, I realised that it was blood.

PJ looked terrified. He saw the blood and turned around and ran out of the kitchen. I struggled to my feet to try to follow him.

He pulled open the front door and ran outside where PC Brent and PC Biller were waiting on the front path.

'Hey!' they shouted as he tried to push past them. PC Brent managed to grab his arm.

I stumbled to the doorway and they both gasped.

'What on earth has been happening here?' asked PC Brent.

PJ struggled and tried to get out of her grip.

'Penny, do you want to take him to the car while I sort Maggie out?' said PC Biller.

I could see PJ was still struggling as PC Brent led him down the path.

'It's OK,' PC Biller nodded to me. 'She'll wait with him in the car while he calms down.'

I was still in shock as she led me to the sofa and sat me down.

'Let me get something for that head of yours,' she told me.

My head was throbbing and suddenly I felt very woozy.

'Could I have a glass of water, please?' I mumbled.

PC Biller fetched me a drink and some kitchen roll to press against my head to try to stem the bleeding. She sat with me while I had a few sips of water and took some deep breaths and, gradually, my heart rate started to slow down.

'So can you tell me what happened?' she asked.

I described how PJ had returned to my house and then come downstairs.

'He said he didn't want to talk to the police and when you knocked on the door, he pushed me over and threw a kitchen chair at me.'

'Gosh,' PC Biller sighed. 'That cut on your head looks small but deep. I think you need to go to the hospital and get someone to have a look at it, as you might need stitches.'

'Really?' I said. 'Surely it's not that bad?'

'Really,' she nodded.

'But what about PJ?' I asked.

'What he did is assault,' she told me. 'So he's going to be coming back to the station with us as we need to ask him a few questions. Do you have the number of his social worker, please?'

I nodded. PC Biller passed me my handbag from the side of the sofa. I got out my mobile and gave her Carrie's number.

'We would have given you a lift to the hospital, but obviously we've got PJ in the car,' she said apologetically.

'It's fine,' I said. 'I'll get a taxi to A&E.'

'Is there anyone I can call to come with you?' she asked. 'A partner?'

'No, it's just me,' I smiled. 'I'll be fine.'

'Well, I'll ring a cab for you and stay with you until it arrives,' she told me. 'We don't want you collapsing.'

Thankfully the taxi arrived in ten minutes.

I still felt quite wobbly and my forehead was throbbing, so I was glad that PC Biller helped me lock up the house. As I walked down the path, I saw PJ in the back seat of the police car with PC Brent.

He scowled at me and looked away.

I felt upset and annoyed at myself. I think, deep down, I had naively and stupidly thought I was the one who could make a difference to him and turn his behaviour around.

But I'd been wrong.

TWO

Peace and Quiet

I sat in A&E, my head throbbing and a cardboard sick bowl clutched in my hands.

As I waited to see a doctor, all I could think about was PJ. My phone suddenly rang.

'Maggie, are you OK?' asked my supervising social worker Becky. 'PJ's social worker just called me and told me what happened.'

'He was upset that the police were coming – I don't think he meant to hurt me,' I told her.

'But the fact is, he did,' she said. 'And that's not on.'

I explained that I was at the hospital waiting to be seen.

'Is PJ alright? I asked. 'Where is he now?'

'He's at the police station being questioned for assault,' she replied. 'Carrie's with him and he's fine. You concentrate on getting yourself checked over.'

'But where will he go tonight?' I added.

'Maggie, he'll be fine,' Becky replied. 'You need to focus on yourself.'

Even though I knew she was right, I still felt really guilty. 'But where will he go?' I asked.

'I think the consensus is that he needs to be in a children's home,' she told me. 'We can't risk him hurting another foster carer.'

Even though I knew that was probably for the best, part of me couldn't help but feel that I had failed somehow. PJ's behaviour was not on – he could have really hurt me – but I still wanted to be the person who helped him turn his life around. He'd only been with me for just over a week, though, and I knew I couldn't live with any child that I thought had the potential to hurt me. When an incident like this happened, sometimes you sadly had to admit defeat and accept there was no coming back from it. I hoped PJ would someday get the help he needed, but I knew now that it couldn't come from me.

Eventually, I was called in to see a doctor. Still exhausted after my sleepless night, I explained what had happened. I could see the sympathy on her and the male nurse's face as I explained that I was a foster carer.

'Gosh, it could have been a lot worse,' she sighed. 'Dining chairs are heavy old things.'

Although the cut on my forehead was deep, the doctor felt that gluing it would be sufficient.

'Have you had any other symptoms?' she asked.

'My head's throbbing and I do feel a little bit sick and dizzy,' I told her.

'Did you lose consciousness or black out when you were hit?' she asked.

'I don't think so,' I shrugged. 'I was stunned for a few seconds but I think it was just shock.'

She made some notes on her computer.

'There's a risk that you could be concussed,' she said. 'If you start to feel drowsy and sick then you need to seek medical attention. Is there anyone at home who can keep an eye on you today?'

'Not really,' I shrugged. 'I live on my own.'

'I don't want to keep you in if I don't have to, but I really think you need to have someone with you for the rest of today and overnight, just to be on the safe side,' she added.

'I suppose I could give my daughter a ring,' I told her.

'I think that would be a good idea,' she nodded. 'If you can't find anyone to be with you then let me know and we'll admit you for observation.'

I definitely didn't fancy a night in hospital if I didn't need one. While I was waiting for my forehead to be glued, I sat in the waiting area and rang Louisa.

I'd fostered Louisa since she was thirteen, when tragically both her parents had been killed in a car crash. She'd been with me ever since and, even when she turned eighteen and left the care system, she'd stayed living with me. To all intents and purposes, I loved and cared for her like I would have done if she was my biological child. And I doted on my granddaughter – four-year-old Edie – who she'd had with her husband Charlie. Their flat was ten minutes from me and I saw them several times a week.

'Hi, flower,' I told her. 'Sorry to bother you at work. I'm just at the hospital.'

'Hospital?' gasped Louisa. 'What's happened?'

I explained what had gone on with PJ and what the doctor said.

'Oh, Maggie,' she sighed. 'That's awful. That must have really hurt. Please tell me you're not having him back to live with you.'

'No, I'm not,' I sighed. 'My agency and Social Services agree.'

I explained that the doctor had said she didn't want me to be on my own for the next twenty-four hours.

'I know it's probably too tricky, what with Edie and work and everything,' I said. 'So I'm happy to give Vicky a ring.'

Vicky was a good friend of mine and a fellow single foster carer. She was fostering a little girl called Paige at the moment but I was sure she'd be willing to let me stay over at her house.

'Don't be silly. I'll finish work around three, so I'll get Charlie to come home and look after Edie and I'll come over to you,' said Louisa. 'I'll make us some dinner and then stay the night. Tomorrow's my day off anyway and I'm sure you'd rather be in your own bed tonight.'

'Are you sure?' I asked her.

'One hundred per cent,' she said firmly. 'I'm not leaving you on your own after everything that's happened today.'

'Thank you,' I said. 'I really appreciate it.'

As a single foster carer, it was comforting to know that I could always rely on Louisa. As a nanny herself, she was police-checked anyway, and she'd also been approved by Social Services as my respite support, so she was there if I ever needed her.

It was another hour before I was seen by a nurse to have my head glued, so it was 3.30 p.m. by the time the taxi pulled up outside my house. Louisa was already waiting outside in her car.

'I'm so sorry, flower,' I told her. 'I didn't realise how long I'd been.'

'It's OK, I've only just arrived myself,' she smiled.

She gave me a big hug.

'Ooh, mind my head,' I said.

'You poor thing, it looks really sore,' she sighed. 'You must have been so scared.'

'It all happened too quickly for me to be frightened,' I told her.

'Well, I'm glad you're OK – I've been really worried about you.'

I unlocked the front door and as we walked through to the kitchen, I saw the upturned chair that PJ had thrown at me still lying on the floor.

I went to pick it up but Louisa stopped me.

'It's OK,' she told me. 'I'll do it.'

'I think I'll go upstairs and have a shower,' I said.

I was shattered but I was scared to go to sleep after what the doctor had said about a concussion.

I paused at the doorway to PJ's bedroom. His hoodie and tracksuit bottoms were lying on the floor where he'd left them, as well as some of his schoolbooks.

Louisa came up the stairs behind me.

'It's not your fault, you know,' she said, reading my mind.

'I just feel like I've let him down,' I sighed. 'He's been abandoned by his mum and countless foster carers – it's no wonder he lashes out.'

'You deserve to feel safe in your own home, Maggie,' she told me.

I knew she was right, although it didn't make it any easier.

★

Louisa really looked after me that night. She made me some pasta and, as we watched a film together, I started feeling very sleepy.

'How are you doing?' she asked.

'Honestly, I'm fine,' I told her. 'My head's stinging a bit but I don't think I'm concussed. I'm just very tired as I didn't get any sleep last night, so I need to go to bed.'

'Well, give me a shout if you need anything,' she said.

'Thanks, lovey,' I smiled. 'I really appreciate you being here.'

The next morning, I felt a lot better, but there was one thing on my mind that I wanted to do straight away.

I called the number PC Biller had given me.

'How are you doing today?' she asked.

'I'm OK, thanks,' I replied. 'My head's still a bit sore but much better. I just wanted to let you know that I don't want to press any charges against PJ.'

'Are you sure?' she asked. 'What he did *was* assault.'

'I'm sure,' I said firmly. 'He's got enough challenges to cope with in life, let alone the threat of going to court and a criminal conviction hanging over his head.'

I was adamant that I didn't want him to be prosecuted. What he needed was help, not prison time.

As the days passed, my cut was slowly healing but my heart was taking longer to mend. PJ's social worker, Carrie, had been round to collect his things, which I'd packed into the suitcase that he'd arrived with from his previous foster carer.

'How's he getting on at the children's home?' I asked her.

'He's doing OK,' she shrugged, 'but he was straight back to his old ways unfortunately.'

She explained that he was skipping school and often failing to come home at night, and was sneaking out on a regular basis.

I knew it would be hard for him in a busy children's home. Staff did their best but they worked shifts so there were always people coming and going. There was always a high turnover of workers, too, so there wasn't much continuity for the kids. They were noisy, hectic places and it was often a case of survival of the fittest for the youngsters who lived there.

'He'll be OK,' my friend Vicky told me as we had coffee later that day. 'You just have to pick yourself up and carry on.'

'I am,' I sighed. 'I'm back on the available list.'

Because of the number of children sadly in the care system – in fact, according to Action for Children, every fifteen minutes a child goes into care in the UK[*] – and the sheer demand for foster carers, it was very rare to be without any placements for long. I knew I should be making the most of my free time.

I tried to do all of the things that I didn't normally have time for when I was fostering multiple children: I saw friends like Vicky, went out in the evening to the cinema or to a pub for dinner, and got the house sorted.

'What about Graham?' Vicky asked. 'You can spend a bit of time with him.'

My friend Graham was a physiotherapist and we liked to go for dinner or a drink from time to time. At one point, a few years ago, our relationship became more than a friendship.

---

[*] Action for Children. 'Home', 2025. Available at: https://www.actionforchildren.org.uk/support-us/campaign-with-us/childrens-social-care/a-place-to-call-home/ (accessed 16 April 2025).

However, with my fostering, I'd come to the realisation that I couldn't commit to anything long-term. Also, Graham had family in Australia and he'd been spending more and more time over there.

'Graham is in Australia,' I told Vicky. 'He's gone for three months this time.'

'I thought you hadn't mentioned him in a while,' she said.

'We decided a long time ago that we're better off as friends,' I shrugged. 'We've both got our own lives and we're too busy to commit to anything else.'

'I know the feeling,' sighed Vicky. 'I've been on my own for so long, I think I'd struggle to share my life with anyone else now.'

I knew exactly what she meant. Being a single carer was hard, but I was used to it. There was no one there to share the day-to-day load but I knew I was lucky. I had great support around me from people like Vicky and other friends who just 'got it', plus Louisa and Charlie of course. I was alone but I never felt it, and I was certainly never lonely.

'Well, I'm very envious that you can catch up on sleep,' sighed Vicky. 'Paige is still waking up at six every morning.'

'She's worth it though, I bet,' I replied.

'She is,' smiled Vicky. 'She's healed me.'

Poor Vicky had had a tough few years. She'd been fostering a group of three brothers – six-year-old Grant, John, ten, and Robert, thirteen. Their biological parents were both alcoholics and they'd witnessed domestic violence at home. When they'd first gone to live with her, they'd shown some really challenging behaviour but Vicky had refused to give up on them. Slowly, they'd started to calm down and Vicky had formed a really strong bond with them. So much so, she'd made the decision to take them on full time. She was even about to apply for a Special Guardianship Order, which meant there would be no more Social Services involvement and she would have full parental responsibility for all of the boys until they reached eighteen.

But then one day Robert had told one of his teachers that Vicky had lost her temper with him and slapped him. As with any allegation made by a child, Social Services had to treat it seriously and do a full investigation despite Vicky denying, of course, that it had ever happened – but the boys had been removed from her care and had gone to live with another carer. Heartbreakingly, Vicky had never seen them again.

It was the most horrific thing to go through and it had been horrendous to see my friend so broken. The police had said there were no criminal charges for her to answer but it had taken Social Services months to carry out their investigations. Until then, Vicky hadn't been allowed to foster any other children so she'd lost all of her income overnight. She'd managed to keep her head above water with a loan from a family member and through working in a supermarket to try to make ends meet. It had taken Social Services six months to finally come back to say all of the allegations were unsubstantiated and Vicky was cleared. However, she'd been so traumatised by the whole experience that she hadn't fostered for a year, until she finally took on Paige.

She'd been hesitant about getting back into fostering but Paige had restored her faith in her abilities and given her back her confidence. She was a sweet little girl and she'd settled in really well.

What had happened with PJ was so insignificant compared to what Vicky had been through. But every time I looked in the mirror and saw the scab on my forehead, I felt a lingering sadness. Vicky was right. I'd learnt over the years that I couldn't save every child and I had to put this behind me and move on. I just hoped PJ would get the care he so obviously needed.

Over the next couple of days, I threw myself into getting the house straight. I also had some training to catch up on at my fostering agency, ironically on allegations and how to manage them. I had to do mandatory training through my fostering agency every few years and they also offered lots of refresher courses like first aid and therapeutic parenting.

I was also enjoying a few lie ins, which felt like such a luxury. I was fast asleep one morning a few days later when I was woken up by my mobile phone.

At first, I was confused when I looked at the time.

6 a.m.

I hadn't set my alarm, had I?

But in my groggy state, I suddenly realised that it wasn't the alarm – it was my phone ringing.

I fumbled for it in the darkness.

'Maggie, I'm sorry to disturb you so early,' said a familiar voice.

'Becky?' I asked, quickly coming round. 'Is everything OK?'

'Something urgent has come up and I need your help,' she told me.

She explained that Social Services had called about an urgent case.

'It's a complex one and you're the first person who came to mind as you haven't got any placements at the moment,' she said.

I sat myself up in bed and listened.

She explained that it was a thirteen-year-old girl who had just come into the care system.

'I think the social worker said the girl was called Saskia,' she said. 'To be honest, I was half asleep too, Maggie.'

'What a lovely name,' I said. I didn't think I'd ever come across a Saskia before.

'Do you know anything about why she's come into the care system?' I asked.

'All I know is that she was abducted and taken to Spain.'

'Abducted?' I gasped. 'What, you mean as in kidnapped?'

'I'm afraid that's all I know,' replied Becky. 'She landed late last night and Social Services are keen to get her settled somewhere so they'll want to bring her to you this morning.'

Becky explained that she could be with me as soon as 8 a.m.

'Sorry, I know it's all so early,' she told me.

'That's fine,' I said. 'I'm awake now.'

And just like that, my few days of respite were over and I was facing a new challenge.

THREE

Introductions

After a frantic hour of rushing around the house, I was as ready as I could be. Somehow it didn't feel right using the room PJ had been in, albeit briefly, so I made up the larger bedroom for Saskia. There was a single bed and bunk beds in there, but at least she would have plenty of room.

It was hard when I had the bare minimum of information and I didn't know if Saskia was coming with any belongings. I decided to wait and see. If she didn't have anything with her then we had all day to pop out to the shops.

By 8 a.m. there was still no sign of her or any social worker. Just before nine, my phone rang.

'Hi, is this Maggie?' asked a voice. 'This is Zoe from Social Services. I'm Saskia's social worker.'

'Oh, hello,' I replied. 'I was expecting you to turn up at any minute.'

She explained that she was still at the police station.

'As I'll explain later, it's a very complicated situation,' she told me. 'There's a lot of red tape and legal stuff to sort out, and I was wondering if you could perhaps come here and collect Saskia?'

'Oh,' I replied, slightly surprised. 'Yes, of course.'

She gave me directions to a police station around a 45-minute drive away from my house. As I got in the car, my head was spinning. I was none the wiser about Saskia and I had so many questions. Who had abducted her? Was she Spanish? And where were her parents?

Just be patient, Maggie, I told myself. In time I'd get all the answers.

The police station was actually the regional headquarters, so it was a huge modern brick and glass building based on the outskirts of town. I went to the front desk and explained who I was and that I was there to see Zoe.

'Zoe who?' the woman asked.

It was then that I realised that I didn't know her surname.

'It's OK,' I said. 'I'll give her a ring and let her know that I'm here.'

I knew her number would still be in my phone from when she'd called me earlier.

I gave her a quick ring.

'I'm here in reception,' I told her.

'Great. I'll come out and get you,' she said.

The receptionist was sat behind a Perspex screen and I could see there was a door at the far end of the room that people kept coming in and out of.

Eventually a woman who looked to be in her forties with short blonde hair and glasses came out. She was wearing jeans and a jumper and I spotted the Social Services lanyard around her neck. I stood up and gave her a little wave and her face flickered in recognition.

'Maggie?' she asked as she walked towards me and I nodded.

'Yes,' I smiled. 'Nice to meet you.'

'Thanks so much for coming all the way over here,' she said. 'Let's go through to one of the offices and we can have a chat.'

She led me through the door, down a corridor and into a small office with a desk and a couple of chairs.

'Can I get you a tea or a coffee?' she asked.

'No, I'm fine, thanks,' I told her.

I was keen to get on and find out more about the placement.

'What can you tell me about Saskia?' I asked. 'My supervising social worker didn't have much information at all.'

'Neither did we,' she said. 'I was the out-of-hours social worker on duty last night and I got a call from the police in the early hours of this morning.'

'Gosh, you've had quite the shift,' I said.

I knew she should have finished for the day by now.

'It's been a long night,' she nodded, smiling.

She told me everything that she knew so far. She explained that four months ago, Saskia had been abducted by her mother Rosa and taken to Spain.

'Her own mum kidnapped her?' I gasped. 'Why on earth would she do that?'

'Rosa and Saskia's dad, James, are apparently going through a very acrimonious divorce and a bitter custody battle,' Zoe told me. 'Before this, the family court had temporarily ordered that Saskia spend equal time with each parent.'

Another custody hearing was due to be held in a few months' time.

But, without James's permission, Rosa had taken Saskia to live in Spain.

'Is she Spanish?' I asked.

'Rosa was born in Spain but she's lived most of her life in the UK, and Saskia was born here and has a British passport,' she replied.

Zoe explained that James had had an inkling Rosa might have gone to Spain and he and his lawyer reported it to the police, who had alerted Interpol. Interpol had issued what they called a 'yellow notice', which was circulated to other countries to flag that Saskia was a missing British child. They also issued a 'red notice' for Rosa, which flagged that she had abducted a child and that there was a warrant out for her arrest. This meant alerts had been issued at all airports and ports.

'That poor man must have been going out of his mind with worry,' I sighed.

'For months, James didn't hear anything,' added Zoe. 'Then last week the Spanish police got in touch to say they had Rosa and Saskia in custody.'

They'd been detained at Barcelona Airport trying to get an internal flight to Majorca. Now they'd been returned to the UK under the Hague Convention, an international law that states children abducted by one of their parents and taken abroad must be returned to their home country.

'Last night they were put on a plane back to the UK,' added Zoe.

She went on to explain that the police had been waiting to arrest Rosa on suspicion of child abduction as soon as she'd stepped off the plane and they'd been taken to the police station.

'Do we know why Mum abducted her?' I asked.

'I haven't had chance to speak to her yet but I'm assuming that it was because she didn't want her ex to get custody. Rosa's being held by the police and will be questioned later,' she told me.

'And how's Saskia?' I asked.

'Extremely quiet,' shrugged Zoe. 'She's hardly said a word since I've been here.'

'Poor girl. She's probably exhausted if they landed in the middle of the night and she's been here since then.'

Zoe said the police had taken a statement from Saskia and they'd got a doctor to check her over.

'There was nothing specifically wrong but she said that Saskia was quite underweight for her age and height,' she told me. 'I get the impression that cash was tight for Rosa and they've been travelling around Spain for the past few months to try to avoid detection, so they've constantly been on the move.'

I really felt for Saskia. There had obviously been a lot of chaos and instability in her life over the past few months and it must have been really unsettling for her.

'How come she's not going to live with her dad?' I asked. 'Surely he wants her back after all those months searching for her?'

Zoe hadn't mentioned any concerns about neglect so I was confused as to why Saskia had suddenly been taken into care and not just returned to live with James.

'That was what was going to happen,' she said. 'The police got her in the car and were driving her to her dad's house. But when they told her where they were going, apparently she became absolutely hysterical. I spoke to the officers who took her and they said she was kicking and screaming and shouting: "Don't leave me here. Please don't leave me."'

Zoe explained that her reaction had sparked enough concern that the officers had taken her back to the police station and called Social Services.

'So, we needed to find a foster placement for her ASAP while we talk to both parents to try and build up some sort of picture of the situation,' said Zoe. 'We just need a little bit of time to speak to all three of them and determine what the situation is and why Saskia kicked up such a fuss about going back to live with her dad.'

She added that before Rosa had kidnapped Saskia, they had a fifty-fifty custody split so Saskia spent alternate weeks with each parent.

'I wonder what happened that made Mum take her to Spain?' I questioned.

'At this point in time, we don't know,' replied Zoe. 'And their custody battle is ongoing. But with Rosa now facing up to seven years in prison for child abduction, it might be that the family court eventually gives custody to James.'

'And how's he reacted to Saskia being taken into care?' I asked.

'Understandably, he's not very happy,' she sighed. 'He and his lawyer have been on the phone to Brian, my manager, several times already today demanding that we return Saskia to him immediately, but Brian's been trying to explain to him that it's not as simple as that. It might be that Saskia only spends one or two nights with you, Maggie, but we need to iron out some concerns first.'

'No problem,' I replied.

There was still so much I wanted to know. Had Saskia been happy with her mum in Spain? How did she feel about coming back to the UK?

'Has Saskia said anything about why she didn't want to go and live with her dad?' I asked.

'We haven't got round to having those discussions yet,' Zoe told me. 'The poor kid looks so overwhelmed and exhausted, we felt all of that could wait.'

I nodded. Becky had been right – it was a complicated and puzzling situation.

'I completely understand,' I told her. 'I don't know if Becky explained, but I don't have any other placements at the moment so I'm happy to have Saskia until you know more.'

'Thank you,' she said. 'I think the main priority right now is probably a shower, some food and a good night's sleep.'

'Is she upset?' I asked.

'Not really. As I say, she's just been so quiet,' added Zoe. 'By all accounts from the police, her mum is the opposite. She's been extremely agitated since they arrested her.'

I still couldn't get my head around what would make a mother kidnap her own child and take her abroad.

There was clearly a lot more digging to be done and questions to be asked. My priority was to give Saskia somewhere safe, warm and comfortable to stay while it was all being sorted out.

'Shall I take you to meet her?' asked Zoe.

'Yes please,' I said.

We walked down the corridor past several doorways until we got to a larger room. Glancing through the glass, it looked like a meeting room.

'Saskia's in here with a police officer,' Zoe told me.

As we walked in, a younger woman in her twenties wearing a white shirt and black trousers was sitting on one of the chairs.

Next to her, slumped on the table with her head in her hands, was a girl. She was dressed in scruffy shorts, a T-shirt and sandals – clothing not really appropriate for the chilly October morning outside. She had a grey blanket wrapped round her shoulders that looked like one the police had given her.

As Zoe and I walked towards her, she looked up at us. She had long straggly brown hair and green-blue eyes with dark shadows under them. She looked absolutely shattered.

'Saskia, this is Maggie,' Zoe told her gently. 'This is the lady I was telling you about, who you're going to go and stay with tonight.'

'Hi, Saskia,' I smiled. 'It sounds like you've had a really long night. You must be so tired. Shall we go back to my house and get you freshened up and have something to eat?'

She just stared up at me with exhausted, blank eyes.

'Maggie, Saskia's got a case with her,' Zoe told me. She gestured to a battered old brown suitcase in the corner.

'Great,' I said. 'I can put that in my car.'

'What, we're going now?' Saskia suddenly asked.

Zoe nodded.

'What about my mum?' she asked.

'Your mum's still talking to the police at the moment, but we'll try and arrange for you to see her as soon as possible,' said Zoe. 'And your dad too.'

Saskia didn't say a word, but I was sure I saw her flinch at the mention of 'Dad'.

I had a very quick chat to Zoe before we left.

'What about school?' I asked in a low voice.

'Let's not worry about school right now, until we know more,' she replied. 'We haven't even got round to talking or thinking about that.'

'I understand,' I nodded.

Zoe was right about Saskia being quiet. She didn't say a word on the drive home. She wasn't asleep but she stared out of the window the entire journey.

When we got in, I showed her the bedroom where she would be sleeping. She looked around with wide eyes.

'You've got a choice,' I told her. 'You can sleep in either of the bunk beds or the single bed, whatever you'd prefer.'

'This is fine,' she shrugged, going over to the single bed and sitting down.

'Do you want any help unpacking your suitcase?' I asked her.

She shook her head.

I showed her the bathroom and how the shower worked and got her out some clean towels as well as a new toothbrush, just in case she didn't already have one.

'Are you hungry?' I asked her and she nodded.

I went downstairs and made her a bacon sandwich, which she wolfed down hungrily. But as she sipped on her orange juice, I could see her eyes were getting heavy and starting to close.

'You must be absolutely shattered,' I told her. 'Why don't you go and have a nap?'

'But I need to have a shower and unpack,' she said wearily, and I wondered how many times she'd had to unpack somewhere new over the past few months.

'You can have one later when you wake up,' I suggested. 'And don't worry about unpacking for now. It can all wait.'

She looked so exhausted, I felt she just needed to sleep.

'When can I talk to my mum?' she asked, sitting down on her bed once we'd headed upstairs.

'I'm not sure,' I told her. 'I don't think the police have finished speaking to her yet, but I'm sure Zoe will ring me and let me know.'

She nodded.

I rummaged through the big cupboard on my landing to find Saskia some pajamas as hers were still in her case. I walked back into the bedroom to find her curled up on the bed, already fast asleep.

'Oh, lovey,' I whispered.

I noticed for the first time how tanned her arms and legs were from the Spanish sun.

As gently as possible so as not to disturb her, I pulled the duvet back and tucked it around her. She briefly murmured then settled back down.

The first few hours and days with a new child are all about getting them settled. I always tried to keep things slow, steady and calm in a bid to not make them any more anxious than they already were coming to a new place with strange people. There were so many things I wanted to ask Saskia but I didn't want to bombard her with too many questions yet.

She'd been through enough in the past twenty-four hours and, for now, it could all wait.

FOUR

A Reunion

The following morning, Zoe rang me.

'How's Saskia?' she asked. 'Is she settling in OK?'

I said that she seemed fine but that she was still very quiet.

'Has she said anything about either of her parents?' she added.

'Nothing,' I told her. 'And I haven't pushed her.'

So many people had been talking to Saskia, including Social Services and the police. She'd been through a traumatic ordeal and I wanted to leave her be for a day or two. I wanted my house to be a safe space for her, so I didn't want her to feel forced to tell me anything. At this point in time, I was just another stranger to her in the blur of the last twenty-four hours.

Zoe also had an update for me.

'I've arranged a contact session with James – Saskia's dad – tomorrow,' Zoe told me.

'Wow, that was quick,' I said with surprise.

There was always a high demand for contact centres so it usually took several days or even weeks to find an available slot.

'He and his lawyer haven't been off the phone since Saskia got back yesterday,' she sighed. 'He's very persistent and his lawyer was threatening my manager with all sorts of legal action if James wasn't able to see Saskia ASAP.'

Threatening legal action sounded a bit over the top but part of me could understand his desperation to see his daughter for the first time in months.

'I'll come round this morning and tell Saskia about it,' said Zoe.

She was on my doorstep an hour later.

'She's in the kitchen,' I told Zoe in a low voice. 'She had a good sleep last night.'

Saskia had woken up at 10 a.m., so she'd had a decent lie-in. After everything she'd been through the previous day, I knew she needed the sleep. I'd put cereals on the table for her to have whenever she came down, and she was just finishing off some toast when Zoe arrived.

I wasn't sure how Saskia was going to take the news about contact, especially as the police had said how hysterical she'd become when they'd told her they were taking her to her dad's house.

'Do you think she'll kick up a fuss about it again?' I asked Zoe.

'We'll have to wait and see,' she said.

There was so much about Saskia that we still didn't know.

She was sitting at the table and looked up as Zoe and I walked into the kitchen. I put the kettle on as Zoe sat down beside her.

'I've got some good news,' she told her. 'We've arranged for you to see your dad tomorrow.'

I waited for her to kick off, but she didn't say anything or show any reaction.

'It will be at a place that we call a contact centre,' Zoe explained to her. 'It's a building owned by Social Services with lots of rooms in which you can spend time with your dad and just chat and chill out.'

'I'm sure you've got lots to talk about as you haven't seen him for so long,' I added.

Saskia was still silent.

'Is that OK?' Zoe asked. 'Maggie will drive you there in the morning.'

'But what about my mum?' Saskia said in a quiet voice. 'When can I see her?'

'Your mum's still talking to the police, but I'll arrange for you to see her as soon as you can,' Zoe told her.

Thankfully, Saskia seemed to have taken the news a lot better than I'd expected.

Zoe had to rush off to a meeting so she didn't have time to stay for a cup of tea.

'She seemed OK with that,' she said as I walked her to the front door.

'She took it *too* well, perhaps,' I sighed. 'What if she refuses to get in my car tomorrow?'

'If she gets very distressed or says that she doesn't want to come, then you'll just have to ring me and let me know,' said Zoe.

But for the rest of the day, Saskia seemed fine. She spent time in her bedroom or watched TV. I didn't push her to go out or do anything, as I knew she must still be exhausted after everything that had unfolded the day before.

That night, I persuaded her to watch a film with me. We sat down on the sofa together. I hadn't pushed her to talk about anything all day but I wanted to try and gauge how she was feeling.

'How are you feeling about seeing your dad after so many months?' I asked her.

Saskia shrugged and continued staring at the screen.

'Are you looking forward to it?'

'Sort of,' she shrugged, without making eye contact.

Around half an hour into the film, I glanced across at her. In the flicker of the light from the TV, I noticed something glistening in the palm of her hand.

I stared at it for a minute until I realised with a shock that it was blood.

'Lovey, what on earth's happened?' I asked her.

I turned on the big light and Saskia looked shocked as she glanced down at her hand. There were several little cuts – she must have been digging her fingernails so hard into her palm, she'd drawn blood.

'Oh, flower, let me clean that up for you and put a bandage round your hand. You don't want that getting infected.'

'Thank you,' she said, looking embarrassed. She must have genuinely not realised what she was doing.

As I patted her hands with damp cotton wool pads, I felt a bubble of worry in my stomach. In the past, I'd had children do things like this to themselves and it was always a sign of anxiety. I knew it was something I needed to keep a close eye on.

What was going on in her mind?

That night I went to bed filled with worry about contact the next morning. Saskia hadn't said it in so many words, but I was getting the sense there was more to her and her dad's relationship than met the eye.

However, much to my relief, Saskia seemed to sleep well and the next morning she was quiet but appeared to be OK.

In the more than twenty years that I'd been fostering, I thought I'd been to every contact centre in the local area, but the one we were heading to that morning was a new one to me.

It was a good fifty-minute drive and as I pulled up outside the centre, I was rather underwhelmed by the place. There was no car park and it was an eighties-looking brick building squeezed into the middle of a large housing estate. It had mirrored windows that meant you couldn't see inside and I noticed what looked like a security guard having a cigarette outside.

I turned around to Saskia.

'OK?' I asked.

She nodded, but her expression told me differently. Her face was scrunched up with worry and I could see the way she was nervously picking at the bandage I'd put on her hand.

'Remember, this is just what we call a contact visit, so you won't be going home with your dad today,' I told her. 'It's just a chance to spend time with him and catch up.'

She nodded and I saw a tiny flicker of relief cross her face before it returned to a worried expression.

We got out of the car and wandered across the road towards the entrance.

'Oh, he's already here,' gasped Saskia. 'That's his car,' she said, pointing to a slick black Mercedes with a personalised number plate.

I didn't know much about cars, but I knew enough to recognise that it was a very expensive one.

Sometimes the social worker arranged it so I wouldn't have to bump into birth parents at contact centres. Normally I got there before them, so I was out of the way by the time they arrived. Sadly, but some might say understandably, a lot of parents saw me as the 'enemy', or as part of the system that had taken their child away from them. In these circumstances it was always uncomfortable for them and for me if we bumped into each other, and sometimes birth parents would get aggressive with me. Other birth parents had a totally different attitude and were desperate to meet me and see the person who was looking after their child.

Zoe had already told me that James was keen to meet.

'He explicitly asked several times if you were going to be there, as he wanted to talk to you,' she'd said when she'd called me.

'That's absolutely fine,' I'd said. 'I'm more than happy to have a chat with him.'

From what I knew so far, I felt sorry for James. His daughter had been forcibly taken away from him and he hadn't seen her for over four months. I wouldn't have wished that on any parent.

As I walked up to the entrance of the contact centre, Saskia lagged behind me.

'Are you sure you're OK?' I asked her.

She'd been so quiet all the way here. I thought perhaps she was worried about seeing her dad after so long.

'It's not your fault, you know,' I told her. 'Your dad won't blame you for going to Spain.'

She nodded but still didn't look convinced.

It was a centre with a secure entrance so I pressed the buzzer, showed the receptionist my ID and signed us in. Once she was happy, she pressed a button and a second set of doors opened and we walked into the reception area.

I was confused to see two men in expensive-looking tailored suits standing with Zoe.

One of them turned to us as soon as we walked in.

'Saskia, darling,' he said in a very well-spoken voice. 'My God, it's so good to see you.'

He was tall and very well groomed, with slicked-back dark hair and shiny brown leather shoes.

Saskia just stood there.

'Come and give your daddy a cuddle.'

He came over to her.

'I've missed you so much, my darling,' he told her, stroking her hair.

She froze like a statue as he touched her.

Then he turned to Zoe. 'This is my lawyer, Harry Chambers,' he said, gesturing to the other man in the suit next to him.

'Nice to meet you,' Harry said, shaking Zoe's hand in a businesslike manner. 'As James's legal representative, I'm here to facilitate Saskia being returned to his care as soon as possible.'

'Absolutely,' nodded James. 'I've had months of turmoil and uncertainty while that mad bitch of an ex of mine went on the run with my daughter. It's a complete outrage that she's not been returned to me immediately. I'm hoping you're going to tell me that Saskia has brought her things so I can take her straight home today.'

Zoe looked as taken aback as I felt.

'Mr Bradbury, this is a contact session, not a family court hearing,' she told him. 'This is a chance for you to spend time with your daughter who, as you point out, you haven't seen for months. We're more than happy to have those discussions with you but I'm afraid now isn't the time or the place.'

James scowled at her. He clearly didn't like being told what to do.

I was also very conscious of Saskia standing there listening to her dad rant on about her mother.

Zoe had obviously had the same thought. She turned to me. 'Do you and Saskia want to go into the contact room and James and I will come through shortly?'

I hadn't even had time to introduce myself to him yet but I thought it was best to get Saskia out of the way. We walked into the empty contact room and sat down. But James had such a loud, booming voice, we could still hear every word he was saying out in reception.

'I'd like Harry to stay with me too,' said James.

'As I explained before, this is a contact session and you don't need legal representation,' said Zoe, clearly getting frustrated. 'I'm happy to call my manager to come and reiterate that to you. It's purely and simply a chance for you to spend time with Saskia.'

'Well, I'm disgusted by the way this has all been dealt with,' said James irritably. 'As soon as she stepped foot back into this country, I should have been given full custody of my daughter. It's degrading having to see her for an hour at a time in this dump of a place. I'm not the kind of a man who has a child in care.'

I glanced over at Saskia, who looked deeply uncomfortable.

'Can I get you a drink, flower?' I asked. 'I can get you a water or a juice?'

'No thanks,' she said, looking down at the floor.

I could hear from the tone of Zoe's voice that she was quickly losing patience with James. 'I'm afraid this is what Social Services have decided is the best solution for Saskia while we assess the situation.'

James snorted. 'What the hell is there to assess? I can't imagine any sane person would want to give custody to a woman who has a long history of mental illness and who kidnapped her own daughter and took her abroad, just to get back at me because I didn't want to be married to her any more. Surely it's in everyone's best interests to give her to her father, who can provide her with a beautiful home, a private school and everything she wants in life? Surely there's nothing to assess?'

'As I said before, James, this isn't the time or the place to have this discussion,' Zoe told him firmly. 'Do you want to go ahead with this contact session or do I have to call security to escort you out of the building?'

I could see the security guard out of the window making his way back in.

There was a pause.

'Yes, I do want to go ahead with the session,' replied James, slightly sheepishly, after a pause.

'Right then, let's go through and see Saskia,' said Zoe, clearly relieved.

'I'll call you later, Harry,' I heard James say to his lawyer, before he and Zoe walked into the room.

I felt Saskia stiffen up next to me.

'Sorry, my princess,' he said to Saskia. 'I'm all yours now.'

Then he looked at me. 'Do you work here?' he said.

'Sorry, Maggie's a foster carer,' Zoe told him. 'She's who Saskia is staying with, at her house, until we sort everything out.'

'Oh, so you're the woman who's got my daughter,' he said, looking me up and down.

There was something about him that made me feel deeply uncomfortable.

He proceeded to fire questions at me – where did I live? How many bedrooms did my house have? How big was my garden? Did Saskia have her own room?

I looked over at Zoe, unsure of what to say.

'And how many others do you have living in this children's home?' he added.

I felt as if he was looking down his nose at me.

'It's not a children's home,' I told him. 'I'm a foster carer and it's my own home, where I live. I'm allowed to foster up to three children at a time – sometimes more if I have permission. However, Saskia's the only child I have living with me at the moment, but that may change.'

He nodded and turned to Zoe.

'I'd like to go and see this foster home,' he said. 'I want to know where my daughter's living.'

It wasn't unusual to have birth parents visiting my house. Sometimes they visited it before their children did. Sometimes, depending on the case and the circumstances, I held contact sessions there. However, given James's condescending and sneery attitude, my hackles were up.

'You'll need to talk to Zoe about that after contact,' I said, being as non-committal as I could.

What I would have really liked to have said was, *with your attitude, mate, you're not coming anywhere near my house*, but I had to appear co-operative.

Half an hour into the session, Saskia was still just sitting there.

'Why don't I go and make us all a drink while you chat to Saskia?' said Zoe, getting up.

It was the prompt that James needed.

'Sorry, my darling,' he smiled, turning to her. 'So, what did you do when you were in Spain?'

'We travelled around,' she told him. 'It was nice and sunny.'

'Did you go to school?' he questioned and Saskia shook her head.

'Mum taught me,' she replied. 'I did lessons with her.'

James laughed. 'I don't think you'd have learnt much from her,' he scoffed.

'I liked it,' replied Saskia. 'It was fun.'

Zoe came back in with a tray of drinks, but James turned his nose up when he saw the instant coffee in plastic cups.

'Is Saskia going to be returning to school now she's back?' he asked Zoe and me.

'Maggie was going to take her later today to enrol in the local secondary,' Zoe told him.

'Yes, there's a good comprehensive near me and they will make space in Year 9 for her,' I nodded.

James looked horrified.

'That won't be necessary,' he said. 'Saskia has always gone to private school and I'm happy to continue paying the fees.'

'Well, if that's what you'd prefer then we can definitely look at that option,' Zoe told him.

'Once we sort all of this mess out and she's back with me, then she'll be going back there anyway,' he stated.

'And I'm assuming my ex won't be seeing her?' he asked Zoe.

Saskia stiffened, but didn't say a word.

'We can talk about that later,' Zoe replied, keen not to have this conversation in front of Saskia.

'Oh, please God, don't tell me she is?' James sighed. 'Why would you let her see Saskia when she's in danger of running off with her again?'

'Mr Bradbury, any contact session with Saskia's mother will be at a secure centre like this one,' Zoe told him.

'I can't believe that can happen,' he sighed. 'I'm going to have to speak to Harry about that.'

Just then, James's phone rang. He looked down at it.

'I'm going to have to take this,' he said. 'It's work.' As he answered, he got up and walked out of the room.

Throughout all of this, Saskia had continued to look anxious.

'Why don't we play a game until your dad gets back?' I suggested cheerily.

There was a pack of cards on the table so we had a game of 'Go Fish', though I could tell Saskia was distracted.

James still hadn't come back in and we could hear him through the window, pacing up and down outside as he took his work call.

We had another game of cards. Zoe glanced up at the clock. It was coming up to an hour and soon we'd have to leave the contact room as it was booked for another family. In that entire sixty minutes, James had only spent five of them actually talking to Saskia, if that.

Zoe looked at her watch.

'I'm afraid we're going to have to leave now,' she said.

'We can wait in reception to say bye to your dad,' I told Saskia.

'It's OK,' shrugged Saskia. 'His work calls are very long.'

Just as we were about to leave, James came through the door.

'I'm afraid the session is over now,' Zoe told him. 'The room is booked for another family.'

'Surely not?' he huffed, looking at his watch. 'I just had to take a quick work call.'

'I'm going to take Saskia back now,' I said.

James sighed. 'Honestly, this is just insulting.'

He went over to Saskia and stroked her face.

'Don't worry, darling, we'll have you home soon,' he told her. 'Harry's on the case.' He leant forwards and kissed her on the cheek.

Saskia didn't react at all, she just stood there, but there was a look in her eyes that I just couldn't put my finger on. Fear? Disgust?

Saskia hadn't been kicking or screaming or creating a fuss that she didn't want to see her dad, but what was crystal clear to me was that she wasn't reacting to James like a child who hadn't seen her dad for months on end.

Something was amiss. I just wasn't quite sure what it was yet.

FIVE

Compare and Contrast

On the drive home, the car was deathly quiet. Saskia didn't say a word; she just stared out of the window.

'I'm sorry you didn't get to actually spend much time with your dad in the end,' I said, eventually breaking the silence. 'He was on the phone a long time.'

Saskia shrugged.

'It's OK,' she sighed.

'Is his job always very busy?' I asked her and she nodded, gazing out of the window.

'Hopefully things will be different next time and you'll get a bit more time together.'

Saskia suddenly turned around to face me.

'What do you mean "next time"?' she asked.

'Zoe's arranged for you to see him once a week at the contact centre. Hopefully he'll have a bit more time to spend with you next week. Is that OK?' I said, trying to gauge her reaction.

Saskia nodded, but she looked like she was going to cry as she turned to stare out of the window again.

It had been a tough few days for her. Perhaps she was still tired after the sleepless night she'd had travelling back from Spain? Then there was all the stress and upset of seeing her mum being arrested and them both being taken to the police station for questioning. Also, I knew from experience that contact was always emotionally exhausting for children. Saskia had had a lot to deal with in the last forty-eight hours.

As soon as we got back to my house, Saskia retreated to her bedroom.

Later on, Zoe gave me a ring.

'How do you think contact went?' she asked.

'I feel disappointed for Saskia,' I sighed. 'James missed the chance to spend any real time with her, which was the whole point of the session.'

'Judging by your face, Maggie, I don't think you particularly warmed to him, did you?'

It was important as a foster carer to be as impartial as you could when dealing with birth parents, but I felt I had a right to say if someone had made me uncomfortable.

'I felt he was a bit over the top, to be honest,' I told her. 'I didn't like the expectation that he could just come to my house and check it was up to his standards.'

'I completely understand,' said Zoe. 'I can assure you that I won't be letting him do that.'

We also talked about the fact that Saskia hadn't kicked up a fuss about going.

'After the way she reacted to the police when they said they were taking her to her dad's, I really thought she might kick off again today,' said Zoe.

'She was strangely disinterested, though,' I added. 'She didn't seem excited or pleased to see him and she almost seemed relieved on the way home.'

However, it was very early days and we needed to get more information about the parents and their relationship with Saskia.

Zoe explained that she was looking into Saskia starting back at her old school. It was over an hour's drive from my house so it was going to take a bit of organising.

'I know it's quite a distance away, so I'm talking to my manager about all of the options,' she told me.

'Well, as you know, I've got no other placements with me at the moment so I'm happy to help out,' I said.

Social Services would often organise a taxi to take children to schools or contact centres if foster carers were unable to.

'I don't expect you to drive Saskia both ways, but perhaps you could drop her off in the morning and we'd organise a taxi to bring her home from school?' Zoe added.

'As long as no other children come to live with me, then I could definitely make that work,' I told her.

We couldn't help but return to how we felt Saskia had been at contact.

'What did you think about the dynamic between her and James?' asked Zoe, after we had finished talking about logistics.

'Her behaviour was quite bizarre for someone who hadn't seen her dad for so long,' I replied. 'There were no tears or hugs or even much conversation between them.'

I'd also noticed that when he'd stroked her hair, she had frozen.

'She was almost robotic with him, I thought,' I added.

I described how quiet and withdrawn she'd been on the way home and how she hadn't wanted to talk about contact.

'It's almost like she's closed herself off,' I suggested.

'It can't be nice for her being in the middle of a bitter custody battle between her parents, so perhaps she's shut herself down emotionally?' suggested Zoe.

I wasn't convinced it was due to that, especially judging by her reaction when told she was going to have regular contact sessions with her dad.

'She looked like she was going to burst into tears when I told her that contact was going to be every week,' I said.

However, there was one thing that Saskia was prepared to discuss.

'She does keep asking me about seeing her mum, though,' I told Zoe.

'I'm working on it,' she replied. She explained that she'd been in touch with the police that morning and they'd confirmed that they'd finished questioning Rosa and she'd been released.

'Have they charged her with anything?' I asked.

'Not yet,' said Zoe. 'They've sent the file to the CPS and they did tell me they think charges look likely.'

She added that Rosa didn't have anywhere to live so the council had found her emergency accommodation. Meanwhile, Zoe was trying to book a session at the same contact centre that we'd been to that morning.

'I think it's good for Saskia to know that she's going to the same place so she's got that continuity,' Zoe told me. 'I just need to check that the security guards are there to make extra sure there's no chance of Rosa absconding with Saskia.'

'Do you genuinely think there's a risk of that?' I asked.

It seemed a secure centre and we'd had to be buzzed in and out.

'She's been accused of kidnapping her own daughter so I don't think we can take any chances,' said Zoe.

Zoe said she hoped to have an answer about contact by the end of the day.

'No problem,' I said. 'Keep me posted.'

That afternoon, I was intending to sort Saskia's clothes out. She'd insisted on unpacking her case herself, but I'd noticed all the clothes she had with her were for warmer weather and they were slightly faded and tatty. I'd been lending her my cardigans and a coat but they were too big for her. Whenever a child came to live with me, they would get a weekly clothing allowance from Social Services so there were the funds to buy her some new things.

I went to her room to talk about it.

'What shall we do about clothes?' I asked her. 'I think you need some warmer stuff.'

'When we went to Spain, we left really quickly,' she told me. 'So I didn't bring anything with me. Mum bought me these things when we were over there.'

'Do you have any clothes at your dad's house?' I asked her. 'Do you want me to ask Zoe if you can go and collect some stuff?'

I knew we'd have to make sure her dad wasn't there if she did this.

'No, no, it's OK,' she told me. 'We don't need to go back there.'

'Shall we nip to the shops this afternoon and get you a few things?' I suggested.

'OK,' she nodded.

*

Saskia was in a changing room when I got a message from Zoe.

There was a cancellation at the contact centre so I've booked a slot for tomorrow with Rosa.

Great, I replied. *Are you happy for me to let Saskia know?*

Yes, that would helpful, thanks, she replied.

I knew the events of the last few days had been a lot for Saskia to cope with. She'd already had contact with Dad, so I was worried that telling her about another session would be too much for her to deal with in one day.

I waited until we were having breakfast the following morning to tell her.

'I've got some news,' I said. 'Zoe's arranged for you to see your mum.'

Her face lit up.

'When?' she asked.

'This afternoon,' I nodded. 'At the same contact centre where you saw your dad yesterday.'

It was the most animated that I'd seen her.

'If Mum isn't at the police station any more, does that mean I can go back and live with her?' she asked.

'Unfortunately, it's not as simple as that, flower,' I told her. 'There's a lot of things happening at the moment so Social Services are talking to your mum and dad to try to get a better understanding of the situation.'

I didn't want to break it to her yet, but if Rosa was charged with child abduction, in all likelihood she could be facing a prison sentence. Later, after lunch, Saskia helped me to clear everything away.

'Are we going to see Mum now?' she asked eagerly.

'In a little while,' I smiled.

She was ready and waiting by the door when it was time to leave.

As we arrived outside the contact centre, I could see Saskia looking around.

'Can you see your mum's car?' I asked her.

'She doesn't have one,' she said.

This time she practically jogged to the front entrance and I struggled to keep up. When we'd been signed in, we went through to where Zoe was waiting in reception.

'Where is she?' asked Saskia.

'Your mum isn't here yet,' Zoe told her. 'But I'm sure she's on her way.'

Zoe got us all a drink but Saskia kept looking anxiously at the door.

'What if she's got lost?' she asked. 'She's not very good at directions.'

'I gave her the address and she's got my number if she gets stuck,' Zoe reassured her.

I glanced at the clock. Rosa was ten minutes late now.

'Why don't you and Saskia go and get settled in the contact room and I'll give Rosa a quick ring?' Zoe suggested.

Please let her turn up, I willed. I knew how devastated Saskia would be if her mum didn't come.

I tried to make conversation with Saskia but her gaze was firmly glued to the door.

A few seconds later, I heard the clunk of the security door and I could hear Zoe talking to someone. Suddenly, Saskia leapt up off her chair and ran out to reception.

I quickly followed her to see a short, dark-haired woman who I could only assume was Rosa.

'Mama!' gasped Saskia, throwing herself into the woman's arms.

They hugged tightly.

'I'm so happy to see you,' Saskia said excitedly.

'Oh, my sweet girl,' Rosa sighed. 'I've been so worried about you.'

'I've missed you so much,' Saskia replied.

They both had tears running down their faces.

It was impossible not to notice how totally different Saskia's reaction was to how she'd been when she saw her dad yesterday.

When the pair eventually pulled apart, Zoe introduced me.

'Rosa, this is Maggie,' Zoe told her. 'She's the foster carer who Saskia is staying with at the moment.'

Rosa turned to face me. She had huge brown eyes and short dark hair, and was wearing jeans and a shirt. She looked tired.

'Thank you so much for looking after my daughter,' she said to me.

'It's a pleasure,' I replied. 'She's a lovely girl.'

Zoe led us all into the contact room. Saskia wouldn't leave Rosa's side and she grabbed her hand. They sat next to each other on the sofa and chatted away.

'What did the police say?' Saskia asked her. 'Were they cross with you for taking me to Spain?'

'You could say that, but you don't need to worry about it,' Rosa told her, giving her hand a squeeze.

'So how have you been?' she asked her daughter. 'Have you been eating enough?'

Saskia nodded.

'She saw her dad yesterday,' Zoe told her.

I saw a look of panic flash across Rosa's face.

'And how was that?' Rosa asked.

Saskia shrugged. 'Mum, please can you tell them that I want to live with you?' she pleaded.

Rosa's face fell. 'I wish I could, sweetheart, but it's not as easy as that right now,' she told her. 'The council has given me somewhere to live but it's just a room. You have to share a bathroom and a kitchen with lots of other people and I wouldn't want you to have to live somewhere like that. And I need to talk to the police again.'

'Please, Mum,' Saskia begged.

'You're better off at Maggie's house while I try to sort this mess out.'

I could see Rosa was close to tears.

'But I want to be with you,' said Saskia, bursting into tears.

'I know you do, Saskie,' Rosa whispered, giving her a hug. 'And I'll do everything I can to try to sort this out, I promise.'

However, I wasn't sure it was going to be very easy.

SIX

Turnaround

When a child first enters the care system, there's always so much to sort out, from settling them in and getting to know them to the endless paperwork and meetings. During those first few days I always feel like I'm being pulled in lots of different directions and I know it's equally as busy for Social Services.

One morning, Zoe rang me.

'I'm going to see James and I thought I'd run a few things by you,' she told me.

She explained that she was going to discuss school with him. Rosa had given her consent for Saskia to go back to her previous school.

'We also need him to agree that Saskia can stay in the care system under a Section 20, like Rosa has,' she said.

Saskia had originally been brought into care under an Emergency Protection Order, but they only lasted seventy-two hours. A Section 20 was where a birth parent gave permission for a child to remain in the care system and agreed to work with Social Services. Social Services preferred this arrangement wherever possible, as it was a positive way for parents to show that they were willing to work with them for their child's benefit. Also, it saved them having to go through the court process to apply for a care order.

'Good luck,' I replied. 'I can't see him and his lawyer agreeing to that though.'

'I'll be explaining that the alternative is we go to the court for an interim care order,' nodded Zoe.

'He *definitely* won't like that,' I said.

'He won't have much choice,' replied Zoe. 'I don't think we know enough yet to just send Saskia back to live with him.'

I didn't envy her having to have that difficult conversation.

'I'll let you know how it goes,' she told me.

Zoe ended up calling in to see me on her way home.

'I was passing so I thought I'd update you in person,' she smiled. 'I think it's always nicer to have a face-to-face chat about things.'

I'd never worked with Zoe before, but I had instantly warmed to her. She was good at communicating and keeping me in the loop, which helped me set expectations with the children in my care.

Social workers have a massive workload juggling multiple cases, and the fact is that sometimes they can become stressed and grumpy. Like any workplace, sometimes you get a clash of personalities. Over the years, some social workers hadn't seen eye to eye with me. They thought I asked too many questions; they hadn't agreed with the way I did certain things or the decisions that I'd made. When it comes to parenting children, everyone has different opinions on how it should be done.

It was still early days, but Zoe made me feel like we working together to help Saskia, and I felt that she wanted to support me too.

'How did your chat go with James?' I asked her.

She didn't look too traumatised.

'To be honest, he was a lot more reasonable today,' she said. 'His lawyer wasn't there and he was quite charming, actually.'

'Really?' I questioned, as that hadn't been what I was expecting.

'I think when we first saw him at contact, he was stressed and in shock,' she added. 'He was expecting his daughter to come home to him and instead she'd been taken into care, which completely caught him off guard.'

Zoe explained that James was happy that Saskia was starting back at school and had offered to have one of his company drivers pick her up from school and drop her back to my house.

'I told him that would be really helpful,' said Zoe. 'I think my manager will agree to it, as long as the driver is police-checked. I have stressed to him that we'll have to see how it goes.'

Zoe went on to tell me that James had given her a tour of the house.

'What was it like?' I asked curiously.

'Huge,' nodded Zoe. 'It's beautiful. Massive garden, big security gates. The kitchen was about the size of my whole flat. Saskia has a comfortable life when she stays with him.'

'James told me how much he'd missed her,' continued Zoe. 'He showed me her room and all of her things.'

I knew a child could have all the material possessions in the world, but that didn't mean they were happy and safe, and not at risk of neglect.

'He might be able to give Saskia a good life materially, but what about emotionally?' I asked. 'I can tell by the way that Saskia is around him that something's not right.'

'James said it's parental alienation,' replied Zoe.

It was a term used frequently in the family courts – where one parent turns a child against the other parent by emotional manipulation.

Zoe explained that James said he and Rosa had had a bitter break-up.

'He said she's very emotionally unstable – she's got bipolar, apparently – and a long history of depression, and he couldn't live with her mood swings any more,' she told me.

'He said Rosa hasn't come to terms with the separation and has been trying to get back at him in any way she can. As you and I know from experience, Maggie, a child is an easy weapon and he claims Rosa has poisoned Saskia's mind against him.'

I sighed. It was so tricky and I didn't know what or who to believe. It wasn't mine or Social Service's job to take sides and get involved in a bitter custody battle. What we did have to do was make sure Saskia was safe and looked after, whether she went back to both or either parent or stayed in the care system. The family court would ultimately have the final decision about custody as long as there were no safeguarding issues.

I knew the one person I would believe was Saskia, but she wasn't opening up to me just yet.

'We need to ask Saskia what she wants,' I said.

'The problem is, even if she says that she wants to live with her mum, she might not be able to,' sighed Zoe.

The other development was that Rosa had now been charged with child abduction.

'The police said that kind of charge is viewed seriously and it can carry up to seven years in prison,' she told me. 'If that happens, then Saskia will automatically have to go back to live with James.'

She would still be able to see her mum, but it would be via prison visits.

'So she could go back to James unless there are any safeguarding concerns,' I said.

'At the moment, I'm starting to think there aren't any,' shrugged Zoe. 'At least major enough ones to keep Saskia in the care system. I suppose Rosa has had four months with Saskia solely in her care to turn her against James if she wanted to. That might be why Saskia kicked up such a fuss about going back to live with him. We don't know what Rosa has told her.'

Depending on Rosa's sentence if she was found or pleaded guilty, they could go back to shared care eventually. But that would be a family court decision and not a Social Services matter. Social Services' job was to decide whether Saskia was at risk and needed to stay in the care system.

'I'm going to have a meeting with my manager today about it,' Zoe told me. 'The constant calls that he's getting from James's lawyer are making him very nervous. We've got another contact session with James in a couple of days, so let's see how things are then and what the interaction is like between James and Saskia.'

'Do you think Social Services will want to do a parenting assessment with him?' I asked.

'Only if there are significant concerns,' said Zoe. 'And at the moment, I don't think there are. It could be the case that we got off on the wrong foot with him and Saskia is simply caught in the middle of a nasty divorce.'

We agreed that Saskia would start back at school the following day. James had given Zoe a pile of school uniforms for Saskia.

'All nicely washed and ironed by the housekeeper, apparently,' she told me, handing me a big bag.

'I wish I had a housekeeper,' I smiled as I looked around my bombsite of a kitchen. There was a pile of dirty washing I hadn't had the chance to bung in the washing machine yet, and a heap of ironing I needed to catch up on.

'Oh, me too,' replied Zoe.

Saskia seemed happy when Zoe called her down from her bedroom and told her that she was going back to school.

'Do you like it there?' she asked, and Saskia nodded.

'I can't wait to see my friends,' she told us. 'It's been ages, since before the summer.'

Zoe explained that I would be driving her to school in the mornings and then she would get a lift back with her dad's driver, who was called Dave.

'Will my dad be there?' she asked.

'No, neither of your parents are allowed to collect you or contact you at school,' Zoe told her. 'All contact at the moment has to be arranged through me and Maggie, and will happen at the contact centre.'

Saskia nodded.

I thought it would be good for Saskia to have some routine back in her life, and I was glad to see her up and ready on time the next morning. We had to leave early because it was such a long drive.

'Don't you look smart?' I said as she came downstairs in her navy blazer and red and navy pleated skirt.

Saskia was quiet in the car but I could see her looking out of the window excitedly as we drove up the long drive to the school.

'That's where we play hockey,' she told me, pointing to a large grass field. 'And there's the swimming pool.'

'It's a lovely old building,' I told her as we pulled up to the main school site. It was surrounded by fields and there were even deer grazing in the grounds.

As it was her first day back in over four months, I took Saskia into the office.

The headteacher, a woman called Claudia Blackmore, was there to meet us.

'Saskia,' she smiled. 'It's so lovely to have you back.'

'Hello, Miss,' she said shyly.

'You're still in your old tutor group and Miss Kensington will take you there now,' she told her.

Mrs Blackmore led me to her office and I filled her in on what was happening.

'Yes, the social worker did call me the other day,' she sighed.

'How have you found Saskia?' I asked her.

'She's a lovely girl,' she said. 'Always very quiet. She's only been with us since Year 8 last year, and it was obvious there was a messy split going on with her parents. Sadly, we're used to that, and it always has to be handled very delicately. It makes things like parents' evenings tricky.

'Dad is very supportive of the school and always makes a generous donation to any charity events.'

Zoe had already told Mrs Blackmore about the driver and the fact that neither parent had permission to take Saskia out of school. I gave her my number and she already had Zoe's.

'Any problems or issues then please give me a call,' I told her.

By the time I'd driven home it was well after ten; I was relieved I wasn't doing the return journey as well.

The day went quickly, and I was keen to hear how Saskia had got on at school. I kept an eye out of the front window when I knew that she was due back as I was keen to meet the driver.

When I saw a sleek black BMW pull up outside the house, I knew it was her.

I walked down the path to meet her. Saskia was just getting out of the car.

'All OK?' I asked her.

She looked very pale and tired and just nodded.

While Saskia went into the house, I stuck my head in the front passenger door. The driver was a grey-haired man who looked to be in his sixties. The car was immaculate and he was smartly dressed in a shirt and chinos.

'I'm Dave,' he told me. 'I've worked for James for many years.'

'Was everything OK with Saskia?' I asked him.

'She was as good as gold,' he nodded. 'See you tomorrow.'

I watched him drive off, then I went to see Saskia who was already up in her bedroom.

'How was your day?' I asked her.

'It was good,' she nodded.

'And was the drive back OK?'

'Yep,' she said, not making eye contact with me.

'Dave seems like a nice man?'

She nodded. She looked ashen.

'Are you sure you're OK?' I asked.

'Fine,' she replied. 'I'm just a bit tired.'

I didn't want to push her any more. I knew it was probably a shock to her system doing a long day at school after being off for four months.

I decided now wasn't the time to remind her that we had another contact session with her dad the following day after school, so I waited until the next morning.

'OK,' she nodded when I told her over breakfast.

'Great,' I smiled, surprised she hadn't reacted more strongly. 'I'll have a snack ready when you get dropped off from school and we can head straight out.'

Saskia seemed more accepting of contact this time. I wouldn't say she was chatty in the car but she didn't appear worried about seeing her dad at all.

I wasn't looking forward to it after the way James had been the last time. He was already there, talking to Zoe, when Saskia and I walked into the contact centre.

'Here she is,' he beamed when he saw Saskia. 'Come and give your daddy a hug.'

Much to my surprise, Saskia walked over to him and James put his arms around her.

'I've missed you, sweetheart,' he told her.

Saskia was frozen to the spot as James hugged her tightly and she closed her eyes.

When he pulled away, James turned to me.

'Maggie, I just wanted to apologise for my behaviour at the last contact session,' he told me. 'I was feeling very stressed and upset and I just wanted my daughter to come home. I know you and Zoe only want the best for Saskia, like me, and I'm truly sorry for taking it out on you.'

'That's OK,' I replied. 'I didn't take it personally.'

As we made to go into the contact centre room, James suddenly paused.

'Oh, hang on a minute,' he said, putting his hand in his suit pocket. 'I almost forgot.' He took out his mobile phone and placed it on the table in reception.

'I'm all yours, darling,' he told Saskia. 'I won't let anyone interrupt this precious time with you.'

I was surprised by this complete turnaround in attitude.

In the contact room, Saskia sat there quietly.

'Why don't we have a game?' James smiled. 'I know my Saskia loves cards. Don't you, Saskia?'

'Yes, Dad,' she nodded.

'Well, I just happened to bring a pack from home with me,' he grinned, placing them on the table. 'Let's play Pontoon. That's your favourite, isn't it, darling?'

She nodded.

'Would you like to play?' he asked Zoe and I.

'No, we're fine,' smiled Zoe. 'You two go ahead.'

A contact worker took over supervising the session while Zoe and I nipped to the kitchen to make a coffee.

'See?' said Zoe as she flicked on the kettle. 'I think we got off on the wrong foot with him.'

'Maybe,' I nodded.

'He's a lot more engaged with Saskia and she's a lot more responsive towards him, don't you think?'

I knew it looked that way, but I still wasn't sure. I just didn't think Saskia looked entirely relaxed or comfortable with him. There was a blankness in her eyes when she was with her dad, like she wasn't entirely there.

Was this a true reflection of the genuine James, or was this someone on his best behaviour, saying and doing all of the right things that he knew Zoe and I needed to see?

SEVEN

Conflict

As the days passed and we slowly got to know each other, Saskia gradually became more comfortable with me. She was a sweet girl and always offered to help out, which was quite rare with teenagers. In particular, she liked to help me cook.

I learnt that she would talk more and start to open up to me when we were doing an activity side by side, like cooking.

'Me and Mum used to make things together in Spain,' Saskia told me one weekend when we were baking some scones.

'What kinds of things did you cook?' I asked.

'We tried to make Spanish stuff like Spanish omelette but that went really wrong,' she replied, smiling. 'Mum got eggshell in it and the potatoes went all mushy.'

'Are you a good cook?' I asked her and she nodded.

'But my mum's not,' she giggled. 'One time, she even burnt pasta.'

'She's lucky that she's got you to help her then, isn't she?' I smiled and Saskia nodded.

'Mum says she has to share a kitchen now with lots of other people that she doesn't know,' she said sadly.

'So, did you like Spain?' I asked, changing the subject.

She smiled. 'It was nice,' she said. 'It was warm and sunny. We kept moving around but there were loads of beaches, and one time we stayed in this lady's house and she let us use her swimming pool.'

'That sounds fun,' I smiled.

'And what about Dad?' I asked. 'Did you ever go on holiday with him?'

Whenever I mentioned James, I could see Saskia's face change. It was like a dark cloud had descended on her and she would close down.

'Sometimes,' she shrugged. 'Shall I put these scones in the oven now?' she asked, obviously not wanting to share more.

Contact sessions with both parents were still happening once a week, and I could still notice the difference between how Saskia was with her mum compared to her dad.

She didn't kick up any fuss about going to see James, but conversation was stilted and polite between them. Saskia kissed and hugged him when he asked, but she was very robotic and stiff. With Rosa, Saskia's body language was relaxed and natural and I could see that she was at ease. They were very affectionate together, and laughed and chatted. There was no laughter with James.

I tried to bring it up with Zoe a few times, but she dismissed it.

'You've got to remember, Maggie, she's just spent four months solely with her mum,' she told me. 'They're bound to be closer to each other.'

As she pointed out, James hadn't seen his daughter in all of that time.

'He's having to get to know her all over again and build that trust back up,' she said. 'So I don't think it's fair to compare. She goes willingly to contact and there is affection between them.'

It was true that Saskia wasn't refusing to go to contact with James, but everything felt very false and stilted to me, like she was going through the motions and saying what James wanted to hear.

Zoe and I didn't attend every session now – a contact worker had taken over. I'd drop Saskia off, then nip out and do some shopping or catch up on paperwork in another room until the hour was over. The notes from the contact worker about James were all very positive. He was affectionate to Saskia and was engaged with her, and she chatted to him.

After sessions with Rosa, she was always very clingy and upset to leave her, but there were no tears when it came to saying goodbye to her dad.

When Saskia had been with me for three weeks, a Looked After Child (LAC) Review was organised. This was a meeting that was held for every child in the first few weeks of them being in the care system. It was a chance for everyone involved in that child's care to get together and talk about how things were going. It was also a chance for them to agree on a plan going forward.

I was going to the review as well as my supervising social worker, Becky. Zoe would also be there along with her manager, Brian. The police had also been invited to give an update and someone from Saskia's school would have been asked to come along. As was standard practice, James and Rosa had both been invited to attend.

The meeting was being held at the main Social Services office in town – a place I was familiar with as I'd been there many times before.

'Are James and Rosa going to come?' I asked Zoe and she nodded.

'Yep,' she told me. 'Both of them said they wanted to be there.'

'Wow, things might get pretty heated then,' I replied.

Zoe explained that she'd called them both beforehand and told them in no uncertain terms that the meeting was about Saskia, and if there was any arguing or bad behaviour between them then they'd be asked to leave.

To be honest, I was dreading it, and on the morning of the meeting, I had a sinking feeling in my stomach as I headed to the Social Services building to meet Zoe. As we walked in, the first person I saw waiting in reception was James. My heart sank when I noticed he was with his lawyer again. Parents were allowed to bring legal representation but it didn't feel as if it was really needed at a LAC review.

'Hello, you two,' smiled James. 'How's that beautiful daughter of mine?'

'She's fine, thank you,' I told him.

As always, I tried to be impartial, but when James spoke I prickled with irritation.

'Just to let you know, Rosa has said she's also attending today,' Zoe told him.

'Oh, we'll see about that,' sighed James, rolling his eyes. 'Her mental health challenges tend to make her very unpredictable and unreliable.'

Zoe and I both chose to ignore his comments, which were making me feel rather uncomfortable.

Becky arrived and while we chatted, I could see James working the room. He was shaking everyone's hand and introducing himself to Saskia's Independent Reviewing Officer (IRO), a woman called Karolina. She had only recently been appointed and I hadn't met her yet, but James and Harry, his lawyer, were clearly leading a charm offensive.

The role of an IRO was to make sure that the child's best interests were taken into account at all times. They were normally someone who worked at a senior level at Social Services but who wasn't directly involved in the case.

'Shall we make a start then?' Karolina asked, and everyone started taking their seats.

'Is there anyone coming from Saskia's school or the police?' I asked Zoe.

'I don't think so,' she replied.

The IRO's job was also to chair the meeting, and Karolina was about to begin when suddenly the meeting room door flew open.

A flustered-looking Rosa stood there. She was dressed in the same scruffy jeans and shirt that she'd been wearing to contact, and her bag was open and overflowing.

'So sorry, the bus was late,' she mumbled breathlessly as her eyes darted around the room to try to find a seat.

I saw a look of panic cross her face as she noticed James.

'Oh, here she is,' he sighed loudly to Harry, seated next to him. 'Better late than never, I suppose.'

'My ex isn't known for her punctuality,' he told the rest of the room.

Rosa looked so uncomfortable and I felt sorry for her. I waved her over to where Becky and I were sitting.

'We can squeeze you in here,' I told her, moving my things along.

'I'll go and get you a chair,' said Becky.

'Thank you,' she nodded gratefully.

Once Rosa was seated, Karolina opened the meeting by outlining why Saskia had been taken into care. Rosa closed her eyes as Karolina talked about how Rosa had taken Saskia illegally to Spain without James's consent. She went on to describe how, after four months, they'd been detained at Barcelona Airport after they were found trying to get on an internal flight to Majorca. The Spanish courts had organised for them to be extradited to the UK under the Hague Convention.

'The police aren't here today unfortunately, but I've got a letter from them detailing what happened,' stated Karolina. 'They say they arrested Mrs Bradbury on her arrival back in the UK at the airport, and she and Saskia were taken to police headquarters.'

She described how, on telling Saskia they were taking her to her dad's house, she had become very distressed and hysterical.

'The police described how Saskia was crying and saying, "Please don't leave me here. Please don't make me go back and live with him,"' added Karolina. 'They were concerned enough to take her back to the police station and call Social Services.'

'That's complete and utter nonsense,' shouted James, suddenly interrupting. 'It's clear my deranged ex spent the four long months she was on the run in Spain poisoning my own daughter against me.'

This time it was his lawyer's turn to interrupt.

'What James is saying is that this is clearly a case of parental alienation,' Harry stated. 'We feel that it's unfair and unjust that Saskia was even brought into the care system in the first place. She should have been returned to James immediately so they could start to rebuild their relationship.'

'Can I be allowed to continue, please?' asked Karolina sternly.

She also outlined the fact that Rosa had now been charged with child abduction.

'I think the plea hearing for that will be in a couple of weeks but the CPS have indicated that a custodial sentence is likely.'

I heard Rosa sigh and when I glanced at her, I saw a tear running down her cheek.

'Good!' boomed James. 'For the ordeal that mad woman put me and my daughter through, they should throw away the key.'

'James, please,' Harry said, holding his hand up as if to shush him.

'Mr Bradbury, I know feelings are running high but this meeting is about your daughter. It's not a chance for you to fire insults at your former partner,' Karolina told him.

I could feel Rosa shaking next to me.

'Understood,' nodded James. 'I'm very sorry. I love my daughter so much and those long months without her, not knowing where she was and if she was safe, nearly broke me.'

'Liar!' spat Rosa suddenly. 'You only care about yourself.'

'Mrs Bradbury, may I remind you too about what you're saying,' said Karolina firmly.

James rolled his eyes and sighed as if to say: *I told you so*.

Becky and I exchanged glances. It was going to be a very long and excruciating meeting if Saskia's parents spent the entire time trading insults.

Clearly keen to move things along, Karolina turned to Zoe so she could outline what had been happening in terms of contact and school for Saskia. Zoe described how Saskia had returned to her old school and, talking to her teachers, seemed to be settling back in well.

'Contact has been happening with both birth parents once a week each,' Zoe said. 'Reports from the contact worker state that Saskia engages with both parents and it's clear she's especially close to her mum.'

'That's only one person's opinion and they're always going to side with the woman,' huffed James under his breath.

Then Karolina turned to me.

'Maggie, how's Saskia settling in at your house?' she asked.

'It's taken a while,' I said. 'Saskia was very quiet and withdrawn when she first came to me. In some respects, she still is.'

I described how at first, I felt that there had been some anxiety around contact.

'It was mainly around seeing James,' I said. 'She kept asking when she would see her mum and they're clearly very close. But it's like she closes down when I ask her anything about her dad.'

When I'd finished speaking, I waited for the barrage of abuse from James. However, I noticed the warning look Harry gave him as he knew that verbally attacking a foster carer at a meeting wouldn't go down well.

'And how are things with contact now?' asked Karolina.

'Saskia doesn't say much about contact with her dad but she goes,' I replied. 'I can see she always finds it very hard to say goodbye to her mum and there's a genuine love and affection between them.'

Then we moved on to talking about school.

'School itself seems to be going very well and her teachers are pleased with the way she's settled back in,' I told Karolina. 'But when Saskia gets home, she seems very anxious. She looks pale and exhausted when she walks through the door and she doesn't want to talk much.'

'It could be her getting used to be being back in the school routine again?' suggested Zoe. 'We know that she didn't go to school in Spain.'

'It could be that,' I nodded. 'Saskia's teachers say she's fine in school, but when she gets home, she seems different somehow. I can't put my finger on it – she just looks and seems so anxious.'

'Well, let's keep an eye on it,' Karolina told me. 'I know I haven't actually had the chance to meet Saskia myself yet, but if it's OK with you, Maggie, I'm going to go to school and have a chat to her there.'

'That's absolutely fine by me,' I nodded.

Then Zoe addressed the meeting.

'Have you asked Saskia what she wants?' asked Karolina.

'I have,' replied Zoe. 'At first, it was very much that she wanted to live with her mum but, in the past few days when I've asked, she's been very vague and says that she doesn't know.'

'Perhaps she doesn't want to be seen to be taking sides?' suggested Karolina.

'Maybe,' nodded Zoe.

Karolina paused for a few moments as she gathered her thoughts.

'There were clearly concerns at first given Saskia's reaction to the police and I feel it was the right decision to get

Social Services involved. But, weighing everything up, I feel as if those concerns have never materialised into anything more tangible.'

She sighed.

'It's not Social Services' job to decide which birth parent gets custody in the divorce,' she added. 'That is ultimately the family court's job. What we have to decide is if Saskia is at risk of significant harm or neglect and, from what I've heard so far, it doesn't seem that way.'

'Mrs Bradbury is still very much able to have contact with Saskia once a week at a contact centre, but with a potential custodial sentence in the future, I don't feel it's right at this time for Saskia to be returned to joint care.'

'Yes!' grinned James.

Rosa looked horrified.

'But this isn't fair!' she shouted. 'My daughter wants to be with me!'

'No, she doesn't,' James told her. 'Even if she did, she can't be with you because you're going to prison for kidnap.'

Rosa burst into tears.

'Taking her to Spain was worth it because it got her away from you,' she spat. 'You disgust me. You don't love Saskia – it's all about power and control, just like it was with me.'

'Mrs Bradbury,' said Karolina. 'You've already had one warning.'

'I don't care,' Rosa hissed. 'It's pathetic! You've all been taken in by his "doting dad" act.'

'Mrs Bradbury!' said Karolina firmly.

'Please don't call me that,' said Rosa. 'I don't want to share the same name as that man.'

Zoe's manager, Brian, stepped in.

'Mrs Bradbury . . . Rosa,' he said. 'I'm afraid I'm going to have to ask you to leave this meeting. You've been warned several times about your manner and we expect you to uphold certain standards.'

He stood up and opened the door.

James smiled and started to slow handclap. His lawyer quickly stopped him.

In tears, Rosa picked up her bag and left. The atmosphere in the room felt very heavy.

'I'm sorry you all had to witness that spectacle but that's exactly what my ex is like,' sighed James. 'Unbalanced and mentally ill.'

'Right, if we could get back to business, please,' said Karolina, trying to bring things back into focus.

Then it was Harry's turn to speak.

'I just want to say on behalf of my client that James is very grateful to Social Services for stepping in and making sure that his daughter is OK,' he said. 'It's clear any concerns about his love and care for Saskia are completely unfounded and a figment of his ex-wife's imagination.

'As you have all seen from her behaviour today, Rosa isn't the easiest person to live with, and James is of the belief that what Saskia really needs is some stability in her life, which is exactly what he can offer.

'Now we've all established there's no reason to keep Saskia in the care system, I implore Social Services to return Saskia to her father, with immediate effect.'

'I don't feel that we can do that right away,' said Karolina. 'Saskia has already been through a lot of change in the past few months. A bit more time will allow Saskia to share any concerns that she has about moving back in with Mr Bradbury and give her time to adjust if she is feeling anxious.'

But Harry clearly wasn't willing to accept this.

'We will expect Saskia to be back at home with James within the next week,' he told Karolina.

'I'm afraid I can't guarantee that right now,' she replied.

'Then we'll see you in court,' yelled James.

EIGHT

Secrets and Lies

As the meeting ended and everyone started to leave, all I could think about was Saskia and what she was going to make of all of this.

'I'll walk out with you,' Becky told me.

We chatted as we got the lift down together.

'How do you think Saskia's going to react to being told that in all likelihood she's going to be going back to live with her dad?' asked Becky.

'I honestly don't know,' I sighed. Saskia was so quiet when it came to her dad, and it was difficult to get a picture of what her life had been like with him.

When we got to the car park, we went our separate ways as Becky's car was on the opposite side to mine.

As I was walking towards my car, I saw a figure in front of me waiting at the bus stop.

It was Rosa.

I could see that she was crying and I couldn't not go over and check that she was all right.

'Are you OK?' I asked her.

'Not really,' she replied.

'That meeting must have been really tough for you,' I told her. 'It must be a really stressful time for you with the court case and everything.'

She nodded.

'So are they sending Saskia back to live with James?' she asked me.

It was really Zoe's job to break the news to her, not mine, but I couldn't lie to her.

'It looks like that's the likely outcome, but it's not 100 per cent definite yet,' I told her.

A tear rolled down her cheek and I passed her a packet of tissues out of my handbag.

'The thing is, Maggie, James is a good actor,' she sniffled. 'People are taken in by the expensive suit and the good manners. But just because he's got money doesn't mean he's a nice person or a good father. He's a master manipulator and a bully.'

I did feel sorry for Rosa; however, my concern was for Saskia who I felt was caught in the middle of this clearly very toxic relationship.

'I know your marriage didn't work out, but this isn't about you two, it's about Saskia and her being safe and happy,' I told her gently.

'I *am* thinking about Saskia,' replied Rosa. 'And I don't believe she's either of those things with him. I'd rather her stay in care than be with James full time.'

'If that's the case, Rosa, and you have serious concerns about his ability to care for Saskia, then you have to tell Social Services what those concerns are,' I urged her.

'Whatever I say, no one will believe me,' she sighed. 'The police weren't willing to listen to me. I don't have the money for fancy lawyers and James has done a good job of painting me as a mentally unstable mother.'

She dabbed her eyes.

'That's why I took her to Spain,' she sighed. 'I could see Saskia was getting more and more withdrawn. I could see she wasn't happy when she had to go and stay at his house. She used to get very teary when the time came for me to drop her off and she'd beg me not to leave her there.'

'Why didn't you go through the courts to try to get full custody?' I asked.

'The family court wouldn't listen,' she sighed. 'They're obsessed by fifty-fifty custody. I wouldn't have had a chance with his lawyers threatening me. In fact, I could have faced losing custody of Saskia completely.'

Rosa described how James had threatened to use her mental health against her if she challenged him for custody.

'It's true that I've struggled with my mental health over the years,' she nodded. 'It doesn't stop me from being a good mum, but I know he would have spun it that way.'

Rosa explained that she was bipolar and had been diagnosed with postnatal depression when Saskia was born.

'I've had bouts of depression since then,' she sighed. 'A lot of it was triggered by being married to James and being unhappy, but I control it well now with medication. But I knew his lawyers would paint me as some mentally unstable person.'

She started to cry again.

'I took Saskia to Spain because I was desperate, and I couldn't see any other way out,' she wept. 'I could see my daughter was turning more and more into a shadow of herself because she was having to live with her dad half the time. And now I've messed it all up,' she sobbed.

At this point in time, I didn't know what the truth was any more, but Rosa was obviously very upset and I felt for her.

'Why hasn't Saskia said anything if she was so unhappy?' I asked her. 'We've all asked her so many times how she feels about going to live with her dad.'

'She's scared of him, too. He knows exactly which buttons to press. He's probably told her what to say or even threatened her.'

'That's impossible,' I replied. 'Neither you nor James has been on your own with Saskia since she came into the care system.'

'Oh, James will have found a way to get to her somehow,' Rosa said vehemently.

I told her how Saskia hadn't really opened up to me much.

'What was it about living with her dad that she disliked so much?' I asked Rosa.

'I don't know,' she sighed. 'I've begged and pleaded with her to tell me, and in Spain we had this conversation so many times, but she wouldn't open up. He's put the fear of God into her. I know my little girl and I know there's something. Some secret that she's hiding from me. What I do know is that she isn't safe with him, Maggie, please believe me. Please do everything in your power to make sure that she doesn't get sent to live with him.'

'I have to go by what Social Services decide,' I told her. 'But if Saskia does have any worries, she needs to share them with us.'

'I really wish she would,' sighed Rosa.

★

That afternoon, Zoe had arranged to come round and talk to Saskia after school.

As always, Saskia looked drained when she came through the door.

'Are you OK, flower?' I asked her. 'You look worn out.'

'I'm OK,' she shrugged.

I'd even had a chat with Dave the driver a couple of days ago about how Saskia seemed on the way home.

'She's always as good as gold,' he'd told me. 'She's a quiet little thing. She just stares out of the window or reads a book.'

I told Saskia that Zoe was in the kitchen and had come to talk to her about a few things.

'Hi, Saskia,' smiled Zoe as she walked in the room. 'Come and sit down and let's have a chat.'

'What's happened?' asked Saskia suspiciously.

'Nothing for you to worry about at all,' Zoe told her. 'We just had a meeting today with your parents and I wanted to tell you about it.'

Saskia looked terrified.

'Were you all talking about me?' she asked nervously.

'We were saying how we all want you to be happy,' I told her, putting a plate of Hobnobs down on the table.

Zoe explained that we'd talked about where she might live in the future.

'As you know, your mum will have to go to court soon for taking you to Spain without your dad's permission,' Zoe told her.

'But that's not fair,' sighed Saskia, close to tears. 'She didn't do anything wrong.'

'In the eyes of the law, I'm afraid she did,' Zoe said gently. 'Your dad didn't know where you'd gone and it meant that he couldn't see you, which breaks the temporary order that the family court made that said you would spend half your time with him.'

She paused.

'So, with that in mind, Social Services were discussing where you might live,' she continued. 'At this point in time, we don't know what's going to happen with your mum's court case. So it was decided that the best option might be that you go back and live with your dad.'

Saskia looked down at the floor.

'Why?' she asked in a small voice, after a pause.

'Because that's what your dad wants and you haven't given us any reason why you don't want to live with him,' Zoe told her. 'If there are no concerns then there's no need for you to be in the care system.'

Saskia looked like she was about to burst into tears.

'Is there any reason, flower, why you wouldn't want to go and live with your dad?' I asked. 'Because now is the time to tell us.'

Still looking down at the floor, Saskia shook her head.

'I can assure you that, whatever happens, you'll still see your mum,' Zoe assured her. 'That won't change, whether that's at a contact centre or a prison.'

'Prison?' gasped Saskia. 'Do you think she really might get sent to jail?'

I put my hand on hers and gave it a comforting squeeze. She was thirteen and old enough to understand, so Social Services had to be honest with her.

'Yes, the police have told your mum there's a chance that she might get a prison sentence,' Zoe told her.

'That's so unfair!' she gasped.

'But we won't know anything definite until she goes to court,' Zoe stressed.

I'd told Zoe about the conversation I'd had with Rosa after the LAC review, and I knew she was keen to confirm in her own mind that Saskia really did want to go and live with James.

'Saskia, Social Services will always take your views into consideration, so please let us know if you have any questions or concerns about going to live with your dad.'

'I suppose it's fine,' she said meekly.

It wasn't exactly convincing, and there was no excitement or happiness there.

'When do I have to go?' she added.

'Lovey, you don't *have* to do anything,' I told her. 'You do have choices. If you've got any concerns or worries about going to live with Dad, now is the time to share them with us.'

'It's fine,' she said resolutely. 'Why do you keep asking me?'

'Up until a few weeks ago, you were telling me how you wanted to stay with your mum and questioning why you even had to see your dad at contact,' I said. 'And when you first got back to England, the police said you were hysterical at the thought of them taking you to your dad's house. What's made you change your mind?' I asked.

'Nothing,' she said quietly, still not making eye contact with me. 'I told you – I'll go.'

'Maggie, I think that's enough,' interrupted Zoe. 'Saskia's told us what she is willing to do, so let's leave it there.'

As she was explaining to Saskia how they wanted to settle her back in with her dad gradually over a few weeks, I happened to glance down at Saskia's hands in her lap. It was then that I noticed blood on her trousers.

'Saskia, your hand!' I gasped.

I could see that she'd been digging her nails into her palm again and her old cut had opened back up.

'Lovey, let me have a look at it,' I told her.

'No!' she yelled, pulling her sleeve down over it. 'It's fine. I'm going to my room.'

With that, she got up from the table and walked out.

'She seemed to accept that OK,' said Zoe. 'At least better than I expected.'

'You really think so?' I asked. 'She might be saying that she's OK going to live with James, but her body language is telling me a different story.'

She was like a knot of anxiety and I wasn't convinced.

'To be honest, there's not a lot more we can do,' shrugged Zoe. 'We've asked Saskia multiple times if she has any concerns or if there is any reason why she doesn't want to go and live with her dad. We're at the point now where James's lawyer has a valid reason to take Social Services to court and my manager doesn't want to risk that. There's nothing to convince us that Saskia is unsafe or at risk with James.'

I felt so frustrated, as I felt something really wasn't right. But you couldn't keep a child in the care system on a hunch.

'OK,' I nodded. 'I understand.'

'I'll talk to James and come up with a way to start settling her back in with him,' Zoe replied.

I spent the rest of the evening trying not to think about it. Saskia hardly spoke a word over dinner and went to bed early.

Just before ten, I was folding some clean washing in the kitchen, when I heard screaming coming from above. I dropped the duvet I had in my hands and ran upstairs.

Saskia was sitting bolt upright. Her long brown hair was plastered to her head with sweat and she looked absolutely petrified.

I sat down on the bed and grabbed her hand.

'What is it, lovey?' I asked. 'Are you OK?'

Her eyes looked right through me, like she wasn't really aware of where she was. I passed her the beaker of water that was on her bedside table and offered her a sip, and slowly the colour started to come back into her cheeks.

'What happened there?' I asked her gently. 'You were screaming and crying out in your sleep.'

'I think I was having a bad dream,' she told me.

'What was it about?'

'I can't remember,' she said, shaking her hand free of mine and lying back down.

'I'm fine now,' she added. 'I'm going back to sleep.'

The next day when Saskia was at school, I phoned Vicky and spoke to her about what was going on. As a fellow foster carer, I knew I could share information with her and that it would remain confidential.

'I'm just not convinced that this is what she wants,' I sighed. 'It doesn't take a genius to see that she's stressed and anxious.'

I told her about the nightmare and about Saskia digging her nails into her palm.

'Something is perturbing her and I think she's genuinely terrified,' I told her.

'I think you're right,' agreed Vicky. 'But I can also see it from Social Services' point of view. Unless Saskia's actually telling them that something's not right, then they can't stop her from going back to live with her dad.'

I felt so helpless letting this happen to Saskia but, at the same time, I couldn't force her to confide in me.

That night I lay in bed, my mind churning. All I could think about was Saskia and everything that had happened. I knew that as the time passed, James's lawyer would start to put more pressure on Social Services to return Saskia to James's care.

Finally, just as my eyes were starting to feel tired and heavy, something suddenly jolted me wide awake.

Was it Saskia having another nightmare?

Then I realised that the noise was coming from downstairs.

There was no mistaking what it was – the sound of glass smashing.

My heart started racing. It was 11.30 p.m.

I reached for my phone to call the police, then remembered that I'd left it downstairs charging in the kitchen.

I couldn't just sit here and let a burglar ransack my house and then wait for them to head upstairs. What if they went into Saskia's room?

Maybe the sound of me upstairs or turning a light on would scare them into running off?

Trembling, I put my bedside light on and crept out of the bedroom door. Standing at the top of the landing, I could see a light on in the living room.

I was surprised, as I would have expected a burglar to force their way in at the back of the house so they were out of view.

Suddenly an awful thought came into my head. *What if it was James?* What if he'd got so fed up of waiting for Social Services to return Saskia to his care that he'd decided to take matters into his own hands and get her back himself?

Surely he wouldn't be so stupid . . .

I'd soon find out.

With my hands shaking, I took a deep breath and pressed the light switch on. The light came on in the hallway downstairs.

'Who's there?' I shouted. 'I've called the police. They'll be here any minute!'

Then I waited.

I couldn't hear anyone. They must still be in the living room.

I was visibly shaking. What if I went in and they attacked me?

My other option was to run down the stairs and straight out of the front door, but then I remembered I'd double-locked it and my keys were in the kitchen. Also, I would never run out and leave Saskia asleep upstairs.

I quickly came up with a plan. I needed to dash to the kitchen, grab my phone and call 999.

I crept down the stairs, my heart thumping with fear. I'd just put my foot on the last step when the living-room door suddenly creaked open.

I was frozen to the spot as a person appeared and I let out a loud scream.

NINE

An Unwelcome Visitor

A person stood there, silhouetted in the light.

I blinked, confused. I recognised that familiar grey tracksuit. I could see that it wasn't James.

'PJ!' I gasped. 'What on earth are you doing here?'

'I don't like the children's home,' he scowled. 'I wanna come back and live here.'

My heart was racing and I was still in shock.

'PJ, I'm sorry to hear that, but breaking into my house in the middle of the night isn't the answer,' I told him.

I walked into the living room and saw the window was smashed and there was glass all over the floor.

'What a mess,' I sighed.

'I did it with a brick,' he told me, matter of factly. 'I thought if I knocked on the door, you'd be in bed and you wouldn't let me in. So can I stay here then?'

The last time I'd seen PJ he'd thrown a chair at me in a rage and sent me to hospital. He was bigger than me and I knew he had a temper. I suddenly felt very vulnerable and

I had to think of Saskia asleep upstairs. I didn't want her to wake up and find that a stranger had broken into the house.

But even though I was scared, I didn't want PJ to know that. I knew I needed to come across as calm and in control.

'I'm really cold,' he said suddenly, his teeth chattering.

'Would you like a hot chocolate?' I asked him.

'OK,' he nodded.

'You sit down there and I'll go and make you one,' I said, gesturing to the sofa.

I didn't want to challenge him or ask him to leave because I was worried that he'd turn on me again. I wanted him to stay calm and think everything was fine. I knew now more than ever that PJ needed way more help and support from professionals than I could ever have given him.

Quickly, I walked into the kitchen. My hands were shaking as I picked up my mobile phone from the worktop and dialled 999.

At the same time, I flicked the kettle on, hoping it would help drown out the sound of my voice.

'I'm a foster carer and I need help,' I said quietly as I got through to an operator. 'Please can you send the police. A child that I fostered recently has just broken in.'

As I gave them my address, my eyes were glued to the kitchen door, terrified that PJ was going to walk in and find me.

'OK,' said the operator. 'We'll send a unit as quickly as we can.'

'Thank you,' I whispered.

As soon as I hung up, I heard PJ shouting from the living room.

'Where's my hot chocolate?' he yelled.

'It's coming,' I told him. 'Give me a minute.'

In a panic, I tipped some hot chocolate powder into a mug and filled it up with boiling water. I quickly gave it a stir before I carried it back to the living room.

'It's here now,' I called out from the hallway. 'I'm just turning the thermostat up so the heating comes on.'

Instead, I went to the front door, quietly unlocked it and took it off the latch. It meant that when the police arrived, they could come straight in.

PJ was sprawled on the sofa where I'd left him.

'It's f***ing freezing in here,' he said.

'That's probably because you smashed a big hole in my window,' I told him.

I put the hot chocolate down on the table.

'This should help warm you up,' I said. 'And while you have that, I'll clean up this glass.'

As I got the sweeping brush out from the cupboard under the stairs, I had one eye on the front door, willing the police to arrive.

I knew all I could do was kill time and try to keep PJ calm until they arrived.

Part of me felt a little guilty at the deception, but I knew I could never have him back to live here now.

'Can I go to bed soon?' he asked. 'I'm tired.'

I needed to stall him, as I didn't want him going upstairs and potentially disturbing Saskia.

'Oh, I need to make the bed up in your room,' I told him. 'I washed all the sheets when you left and I haven't made it up since then.'

That was over five weeks ago. It felt like yesterday that he'd thrown the chair at me but, at the same time, it also felt like so much had happened. I'd been so busy focusing on Saskia that it had taken my mind off what had happened with PJ.

Finally, fifteen minutes after I had called them, I saw the flash of blue lights through the front window as the police car pulled up outside my house.

PJ noticed it too.

'You bitch,' he hissed. 'You grassed me up.'

He threw his mug on the floor and stood up.

He lunged for me just as two male police officers burst through the front door. I quickly managed to move out of the way as they went to restrain him.

PJ tried to run past them, but they grabbed him.

'Get off me!' he yelled. 'I ain't done nothing wrong. I'm just a kid.'

The officers restrained him as he continued to thrash around and swear, calling me every name under the sun.

'His name's PJ,' I told them. 'And he's thirteen.'

'I'm fourteen now, you silly bitch!' he yelled. 'And anyway, what do you care?'

Suddenly a figure appeared at the top of the stairs.

Saskia.

'What's happening?' she mumbled sleepily.

She looked terrified when she saw the police restraining PJ.

'It's all OK, lovey,' I reassured her. 'Go back to your room and I'll come up and explain what's happening in a minute.'

Thankfully she did as I asked. One of the officers marched PJ down the path and into the police car while I talked to the other one.

I explained what had happened – that I was a foster carer and that PJ had lived with me for a while, but that he'd attacked me and he'd gone to a children's home. Although I suddenly realised I didn't know which one.

'I've got the number of his social worker if you need it?' I told him.

'We'll take him back to the station and call Social Services,' the officer replied. 'We can talk to the social worker on duty.'

He also took my phone number.

'We'll give you a call tomorrow and see if you want to make a statement and press charges,' he added.

'I didn't last time,' I replied, looking at the window.

'And look what happened,' he said.

I knew it was something that I needed to consider, but right now I had Saskia to think of.

I breathed a sigh of relief as I stood in the living room and watched the police car drive off. I could see that PJ was still kicking off in the back seat.

I stared at the gaping hole in my front window. I knew I couldn't go to bed and leave it like that. It needed to be properly boarded up to make sure that it was secure overnight.

I already felt pretty shaken after what had happened. I didn't want to be lying upstairs worried that someone else might break in.

But first I knew that I needed to reassure Saskia. I went upstairs to find her sitting on her bed looking terrified.

'Why were the police here?' she asked, her eyes wide with fear. 'Who was that boy?'

'It's OK,' I reassured her. 'They've gone now.'

I explained that PJ was someone that I'd once fostered, but that he'd gone to live in a children's home.

'What's that?' she asked.

I explained that it was a big house that lots of children who were in the care system lived in.

'But he didn't like it there, so he decided to come back here,' I told her. 'He shouldn't have come so late at night and he smashed the window, so that's why I called the police.'

'Will he come back?' she asked.

'No,' I told her. 'The police and Social Services will make sure he doesn't come back here and they'll make sure that he never does it again.'

'OK?' I smiled and Saskia nodded. However, I could see how shaken up she was.

'I know it's late but we've both had a bit of a shock, so do you want to come down and have a hot chocolate with me?'

'Yes,' she nodded eagerly.

We went downstairs. The kettle was still warm from when I'd frantically made PJ's hot chocolate.

By now all the adrenaline had left my body and I suddenly felt exhausted.

'I think I'm going to have to give Charlie a ring,' I told her as we sipped our drinks.

I knew it was nearly midnight, but I couldn't think of any other way to get the window secured tonight.

Saskia had met Louisa a couple of times, but not for very long. I tended to see Louisa on her day off during the week when Saskia was at school, and she hadn't met Charlie before.

She finished her hot chocolate while I called Louisa. As it was late, I wasn't even sure she'd answer.

The phone only rang a couple of times before someone picked up.

'Maggie?' asked Louisa groggily. 'Are you OK?'

'Not really,' I told her.

I apologised for ringing so late and explained what had happened with PJ.

'Oh, I'm so sorry, you must have been terrified,' she sighed. 'What was he thinking? I hope he didn't hurt you?'

'No,' I said. 'Luckily the police came pretty quickly but he gave me a fright.'

I explained how he'd thrown a brick through my living room window.

'Charlie will come round now and board it up for you,' she said.

'Are you sure?' I asked. 'I know it's late.'

'It's fine,' she said. 'We were just heading to bed but he'll throw some jeans on and he'll be with you in ten.'

Charlie was a mechanic and Louisa said he had some old plywood boards in the back of his work van.

'Thanks, flower,' I told her. 'I was too scared to go to bed leaving it like that.'

After I'd hung up, I knew I needed to get Saskia to bed.

'You head back to bed, lovey, and try to get some sleep,' I told her. 'I'll wait up for Charlie.'

'I'll try,' she said.

'Don't you worry,' I told her. 'Everything will be fine.'

I went into the living room. All the glass was cleared away now and I'd thrown the brick in the bin outside.

While I waited for Charlie to arrive, I phoned my agency and explained what had happened to the out-of-hours social worker.

'Oh, my goodness,' she said.

'It's all sorted now and we're OK,' I told her.

I explained that the police had taken PJ away and that Saskia had woken up but that she was fine and in bed now. I knew my agency would tell anyone who needed to be told.

'I'm sure Becky will give you a call tomorrow and check how you are,' she said.

True to his word, Charlie arrived ten minutes later. He knocked quietly on the door.

'Thank you so much,' I told him. 'I was panicking about what to do.'

'I can't believe the little twerp did this,' he sighed. 'You've got to press charges this time, Maggie, otherwise he'll think he can do anything he wants.'

'I'll see,' I sighed. 'He's just a kid.'

I felt really torn. Despite everything PJ had done, I still felt sorry for him.

'I'll board it up for now to secure it overnight,' Charlie told me. 'But I've got a mate who works for a window company, so I'll call him in the morning and see if he can come round and replace the glass.'

'Thanks, Charlie,' I smiled. 'I'm sorry to disturb your evening and drag you over here.'

'That's OK,' he said. 'Louisa was shattered so she was asleep on the sofa and I was just watching TV.'

As quietly as he could, Charlie secured the window while I went up to check on Saskia. She was lying in bed but was still wide awake.

'It's all safe and secure now,' I told her. 'So you try to get some sleep.'

By the time I came back down, Charlie was pretty much done.

'Thanks, lovey,' I told him. 'I owe you one.'

'My pleasure,' he smiled. 'I'm sorry he scared you like that. It's all secure now and I'll get my mate to ring you tomorrow.'

'Thank you,' I smiled.

When he'd gone, I closed the living room curtains and turned out the light. It looked terrible but as long as it was secure, that was the main thing.

However, as I lay in bed, I couldn't sleep. Even though I'd tried to push thoughts of PJ out of my mind, I still felt like I'd failed him. And now I felt like I was failing Saskia too.

TEN

Caught in the Act

The next morning, I still felt a little bit shaky as I walked into the living room and drew back the curtains to see the boarded-up window.

Despite everything he'd done, I couldn't help but wonder where PJ had spent the night and what state of mind he was in.

Thankfully Saskia had managed to sleep and seemed fine and unscathed by the previous night's ordeal. I kept myself busy getting her breakfast and dropping her off at school.

I'd just got back home when Becky called me.

'Oh, Maggie, I heard about PJ,' she gasped. 'How are you doing?'

'I'm fine now,' I told her. 'But I wasn't last night.'

'I'm not surprised – you must have been so scared.'

Becky explained that she'd already spoken to PJ's social worker, Carrie.

'I don't think the children's home is working out for him,' she told me. 'When Social Services contacted them last night, they refused to have him back.'

No other foster carer would take him, so they'd had to apply to the courts for what was known as a Deprivation of Liberty Order. It was something the court could grant if there were no other options for a child, or if they had a history of absconding, which PJ did. It was to keep the child safe from themselves, and others.

Becky told me how his behaviour had apparently deteriorated even further over the last few weeks. He'd trashed his room and destroyed furniture, he'd got into fights with other children at the home, and he'd even attacked one of the workers and broken her wrist. I shuddered at the thought of what he could have done to me or Saskia.

'He spent last night in a secure children's home and I think they've decided that the best option is to keep him there,' added Becky.

Secure children's homes provide a safe environment for vulnerable children like PJ, or kids with complex needs. The ones I'd been to in the past usually had educational provision on site, so they didn't go to a mainstream school, and there was a high level of supervision by workers who were more like security staff. The children couldn't wander around freely in the home – everywhere was locked and they had to be given access by staff. I always felt sad when any child was placed in one of these homes, as it really limited their freedom, but I knew in certain situations that it was the safest option.

'I don't know what to do about pressing charges,' I sighed to Becky. 'I'm in two minds.'

'Maggie, I'm afraid the matter has already been taken out of your hands,' she told me.

She explained that Carrie had said the police were going to charge PJ with breaking and entering.

'Whether you agree to it or not, on the advice of the CPS, they've decided they're going to go ahead with a prosecution,' she said. 'Apparently, someone from the police will be ringing you today about making a statement.'

Maybe it *was* the right thing to do? While I could understand PJ wanting to come back to somewhere he felt safe, the manner in which he'd done it wasn't acceptable. He needed to understand that he couldn't always do exactly what he wanted, and that he wasn't above the law just because he was in care.

'Maybe this will be good for him in the long run?' suggested Becky. 'A bit of a wake-up call?'

'I honestly don't know,' I sighed.

A couple of days later, a female police officer came to take a statement from me. With a heavy heart, I told her what had happened when PJ had broken in.

'I don't really think he wanted to hurt me,' I told her. 'I think he wanted a safe place to go, away from the children's home, but he just went about it the wrong way.'

'That will be up to the youth court to decide,' the PC told me, closing her notebook. 'He's clearly a troubled young man.'

After she left, I still felt a deep sense of sadness and guilt. He was only fourteen. I'd done the best that I could but somewhere along the line, we had all failed PJ, myself included. He'd experienced a childhood full of rejection – first from his birth mum, and then various foster carers, and now a children's home.

It was weighing on my mind, so that afternoon I popped round to Vicky's to have a coffee and talk to her about it.

'I know ultimately it wasn't my decision, but I feel so awful about the fact that they're going to prosecute him,' I admitted.

Was the threat of being sent to a young offenders' institute really the way to help heal that deeply engrained hurt and stop the vicious circle of his behaviour? I wasn't so sure.

'Ideally he needs some therapeutic work to be done with him, such as counselling,' I told her. 'He needs to be able to talk about his feelings of rejection and look at ways he can overcome them.'

'But is a fourteen-year-old boy really going to respond well to that?' asked Vicky. 'If he's not willing to do it, there's not a lot you can do.'

'I know,' I sighed. 'But I hate to think of him in that children's home. It's not what I'd want for any child.'

'Sometimes you just have to accept that some kids need secure accommodation,' replied Vicky. 'At least he's safe there and hopefully it will help to keep him out of trouble.'

I just hoped that if the youth court did send him to a young offenders' institute, it would shock him into accepting help and considering other paths he could take in life.

'I've asked the police to keep in touch with me and let me know what happens to him,' I told Vicky.

'You can't blame yourself, Maggie,' she replied. 'You only had him for such a short space of time.'

I knew she was right. I had to put thoughts of PJ to the back of my mind and focus on the child that I had in front of me: Saskia. Social Services were still very keen to take things slowly, so while they came up with a plan with James to gradually settle Saskia back in with him, life carried on as normal.

One afternoon, I was trying to get organised and prep some dinner when I looked up at the clock. It was 2.15 p.m.

Saskia will be heading home from school soon, I thought to myself.

Then I happened to glance up at the calendar on the kitchen wall and my heart sank. There it was in big letters – *4.15 P.M. SASKIA DENTIST.*

With all the kerfuffle with PJ, it had completely slipped my mind.

When a child first came into my care, it was standard procedure to take them for various check-ups, such as the optician and dentist, as well as a GP if they were younger and hadn't had all of their immunisations yet.

As Saskia had an appointment, I'd intended to go and pick her up from school myself rather than for her to be collected by the usual driver, Dave. The dentist was over the other side of town, close to her school, and by the time she got dropped back, I knew it would be too late to make her appointment.

If I was going to make pick-up time, I knew I needed to set off soon.

I decided to call Saskia's school so they could let her know not to get into the car with Dave and that I would come for her instead. I knew he would potentially be annoyed at a wasted journey, but it was my fault and I would hold my hands up and apologise, so hopefully he'd understand. I realised Dave had my number but I didn't have his, and I didn't want to call Zoe and get her to contact James and get him involved.

But when I called the school office, it rang and rang and no one was answering. I couldn't waste any more time so I decided to set off for school myself. I could pick Saskia up and leave a message for Dave with the school or catch him if he was already there.

I got in the car. But as I got closer to Saskia's school, the traffic was really heavy.

Come on, I thought. *Hurry up.*

I even had to queue to turn into the sweeping driveway that led up to the main school building. As I finally pulled into the car park, I saw a familiar black car going past me in the opposite direction – the sleek black BMW that Saskia was dropped back to my house in every afternoon.

'Damn,' I muttered. I quickly did a U-turn in the hope that I could catch them at the gate or the traffic lights, and I could ask Dave to pull over so that Saskia could get into my car.

Frustratingly, the lights were on green so they drove straight out. They were two or three cars in front of me, but I followed them before they stopped off at another set of lights.

'This is a waste of time,' I said to myself.

They were never going to see me, and I was just going to end up following them all the way back to my house! I was about to pull over to call the dentist and cancel Saskia's appointment when I noticed the BMW was turning left into a retail park.

That's odd, I thought.

But I noticed there was a McDonald's there, and I wondered if Saskia might have persuaded Dave to stop off and get her a sneaky milkshake.

Still a few cars behind, I indicated too and followed them in.

I could see the car had pulled into a parking space in front of an electrical shop. I put my foot on the brake and stopped as I watched a person emerge from a black Mercedes parked next to them, which I suddenly realised I'd seen before.

It wasn't just the car that I recognised.

In absolute horror, I watched aghast as James opened the rear passenger door of the BMW and got into the back seat with Saskia.

A car behind me beeped.

I couldn't believe what I'd just seen. What was happening here?

I knew I needed to act fast and get Saskia out of that car as soon as possible.

I quickly drove past them and pulled into the nearest car parking space. As soon as I turned off the engine, I bolted out of the driver's seat and ran over to the BMW, which was thankfully still there.

I pulled open the rear passenger door.

James and Saskia looked up at me in shock.

'I'm so glad I caught you,' I told them calmly. 'I've just realised that Saskia has a dentist's appointment so I need her to come with me.'

Just like I had with PJ, I wanted to look like I was calm and get Saskia out of the car as quickly as possible without James kicking off or trying to stop me.

Saskia didn't say a word as I leant over and undid her seatbelt.

James looked shocked.

'Come on, Saskia, my car's just over there,' I told her.

I grabbed her school bag from the footwell and practically pulled her out of the car.

James got out on his side and started yelling at me as I put a protective arm around Saskia and shepherded her to the safety of my car.

'I'll have you know I've not done anything wrong,' he shouted. 'I just wanted to spend some time with my own daughter.'

I didn't respond. Saskia looked terrified.

'Just ignore him and get in the car please, flower,' I told her.

She did as I asked, and I quickly jumped into the driver's seat and locked all of the doors.

'I'm sorry, Maggie,' said Saskia from the back seat.

'Don't worry,' I told her as I put the gearstick into reverse. 'We'll talk about this later, but I want you to know that you've done absolutely nothing wrong.'

I just wanted to get us as far away as possible from James.

As I drove past them, James was yelling into his mobile phone. It was only when I pulled out of the retail park that I started to feel myself relax slightly.

'Right, let's get you to the dentist and we can talk about this later,' I told Saskia calmly.

'What? We're still going?' she asked, shell-shocked, and I nodded.

I know it might have seemed odd, but I needed to buy myself time to try and get my head around what had just happened, and to calm myself down.

As I drove along, I checked my rear-view mirror constantly to make sure that James and his driver weren't following us.

My mind was buzzing with so many questions that I wanted to ask, but I knew I needed to handle this carefully. Was this the first time James had got in the car with Saskia, or had he been doing it regularly? What had he been saying to her?

While Saskia had her check-up, I sat on a chair at the side of the treatment room and discreetly texted Becky. She was always my first port of call to bounce things off, so I told her what happened and then explained that we'd gone to the dentist for Saskia's appointment and that I'd ring Zoe as soon as we got home.

She replied straight away.

That must have been a shock. What the heck was he doing in the car with her? Keep me posted and let me know when you manage to chat to Zoe.

Half an hour later, after the dentist had declared Saskia's teeth were fine, we walked back to the car.

'Let's get home and then we can have a good chat,' I told her as I started the engine.

But a few minutes later, Saskia suddenly burst into tears.

'Oh, lovey,' I sighed.

'I'm really, really sorry,' she sobbed as I pulled into a layby and turned off the engine. 'I know you're really mad at me.'

'Listen to me,' I told her, turning round in the driver's seat to face her. 'You've got absolutely nothing to be sorry about. You haven't done anything wrong and I'm not cross with you. It's your dad who's broken the rules here.'

The agreement was that he saw Saskia once a week at a supervised contact session and it was James who had gone against that. Now I just needed to find out exactly what had been going on and why.

ELEVEN

Questions Not Answers

On the drive back, Saskia started to calm down. But as soon as we walked in the front door, she broke down again. I led her to the kitchen, sat her down and got her a glass of water.

'I'm sorry,' she wept. 'I'm so sorry.'

'Saskia, you don't need to apologise,' I told her, reiterating what I'd said in the car. 'I'm not cross with you and you're not going to get into trouble. I just want to try and get to the bottom of what happened before I talk to Zoe.'

'Zoe?' she gasped. 'Why do you need to talk to her about it?'

'I have to, lovey, she's your social worker,' I explained. 'She needs to know what's been happening with your dad.'

I knew I needed to work out exactly what had been going on.

'I don't want to upset you any more than you already are, but I need to ask you a few questions,' I told her.

'OK,' she sniffed.

'Was it just today that your dad got into the car with you on the way home from school, or has he done it before?' I asked her.

'Before,' she nodded sheepishly.

'And has he done it a lot of times or just a few?' I added.

She went quiet.

'Saskia,' I said, prompting her. 'It's important that you tell me the truth.'

'A lot of times,' she shrugged. 'Maybe like three or four times a week.'

My heart sank and I was cross with myself for not knowing this was happening. Why on earth had we trusted her with James's driver in the first place?

'And does he come in the car for the whole journey or is it just for a few minutes?'

'The whole time,' she whispered.

Saskia explained that Dave would drive them to the retail park where they'd meet James and he would get in the car. Then he'd get out around the corner from my house so I wouldn't see him.

'I think Dave goes back to pick him up and then gives him a lift back to his car,' she told me.

It was starting to explain why Saskia was arriving back at my house every night looking so pale, tired and completely drained.

'So what do you and your dad talk about when you're in the car?' I asked casually.

Saskia looked away and wouldn't make eye contact with me.

'Nothing much,' she shrugged, staring off into the distance. 'He just wants to spend time with me.'

From my experience of James so far, I wasn't buying that.

'If you're in the car for nearly an hour together, you must talk about something?' I added.

'I don't know,' she replied. 'Just stuff.'

None of this was ringing true to me.

'Maggie, please don't tell anyone,' Saskia begged me. 'Please don't tell Zoe. Otherwise, Dad will get into trouble and then . . .'

Her voice trailed off.

'And then what, flower?' I asked.

She looked down at the floor.

'Saskia, please talk to me,' I urged. 'What will happen if I tell Zoe?'

She started to cry again. 'My dad said it wasn't fair he was only allowed to see me once a week and he has to be supervised when he's done nothing wrong.'

Something about all of this felt off to me, and I was convinced there were things Saskia wasn't telling me.

But I could tell that she'd suddenly shut herself down emotionally, as she frequently did.

I wanted to try to get to the bottom of what James had been saying to her but I also knew I had to give Zoe a call and let her know what was going on.

'Why don't you go and get changed out of your school uniform and I'll make us a drink and a snack?' I suggested.

'OK,' she nodded, looking relieved.

When Saskia went upstairs, I got on the phone to Zoe.

'I was expecting your call, Maggie,' she told me. 'James has already been on the phone, giving me chapter and verse about what happened and complaining that you've been following him.'

'I bet he has,' I sighed. 'And what did he have to say about why he was getting into Saskia's car?'

'He just said that he was passing by chance and he saw the car and wanted to say hello.'

'What utter rubbish. Saskia's already told me how he's been getting in the car with her most days after school.'

'What was he thinking?' replied Zoe. 'We both need to have a proper chat to Saskia and get to the bottom of what's really been going on.'

'She's really upset about it,' I told her.

Zoe said she was able to come round in half an hour on her way home from work.

'I know she's upset but I think it would be good to talk it through with her today,' she said. 'Then at least I can get her version before I speak to James again tomorrow.'

When Saskia returned, I told her what was happening.

'Do I have to talk to Zoe?' she sighed.

'I'm afraid you do,' I nodded. 'It's really important.'

Saskia went to watch TV in the living room while I waited for Zoe to arrive. She was there within half an hour.

'How are things?' she asked me.

'OK, I suppose,' I told her. 'Saskia's been very quiet since we got back and I feel like she's doing that thing where she just shuts down.'

'Let's go and have a chat to her,' Zoe replied.

We went into the living room and I turned off the TV.

Zoe sat down next to Saskia on the sofa. She looked really uncomfortable.

'I hear it's been an eventful afternoon,' Zoe said.

Saskia shrugged.

'So what's been going on?' Zoe asked her. 'Maggie says your dad has been getting in the car back from school with you quite a lot?'

She nodded.

'And this has been happening every day?'

'Not every day,' replied Saskia. 'Three or four times a week.'

It was reassuring to know that she was telling Zoe the same thing that she'd told me.

'What does Dad need to talk to you about that he can't talk to you about at contact?'

'Nothing,' said Saskia. 'He just wants to spend time with me.'

'And do you like him spending time with Dad in the car?' added Zoe. 'Do you enjoy seeing him?'

'Yep,' replied Saskia, avoiding Zoe's gaze and staring off into the distance.

I could tell by Saskia's reaction that she wasn't being honest with us about how she really felt.

'What will happen to my dad?' she asked. 'Will he get into trouble?'

'I don't know just yet,' Zoe told her. 'All I know is that your dad hasn't kept to what he agreed to do, so I'm going to have to have a chat to him about that.'

Saskia turned to me.

'Maggie, I've got some homework I need to do, so please can I go upstairs?' she asked me.

'OK, lovey, you go and get it done before dinner then,' I smiled.

It would give Zoe and I a chance to chat. It was nearly 7 p.m. now and I was sure she wanted to be heading home soon.

'Do you believe her?' I asked Zoe.

'Well, she told both of us the same thing,' she replied. 'And she's thirteen, not six, so it's not as if she doesn't understand what we're asking her.'

'Something feels off to me,' I said.

As a matter of priority, Zoe was going to organise another way for Saskia to come back from school.

'I've already told James that, as of tomorrow, we'll no longer be able to use his driver,' she told me. 'So I'm going to arrange for a taxi to do the afternoon pick-up.'

'It's OK – I can pick Saskia up and drive her back here,' I replied.

'Are you sure?' she asked me.

'Yes,' I said. 'After what happened today, I'd rather know that she was getting home safely than spend every afternoon worrying.'

It was going to eat into my day, but as I didn't have any other placements at present, I could manage it.

'Thanks, Maggie, that's really helpful,' she said.

Zoe said she was going to speak to James again the following day.

'Let's see if he's willing to be a bit more open with me,' she said.

'Will it change anything going forward?' I asked.

'His flagrant disregard for the rules does raise concerns,' she told me. 'I do think we need to ask Saskia a few more questions and do a bit more digging.'

But at the same time, I was also aware that Zoe was being put under a lot of pressure by James and his lawyer.

'Will you have to let Rosa know what happened?' I asked.

'I think we need to tell her,' replied Zoe.

I suddenly remembered that it was Rosa's turn for contact with Saskia the following day.

'I'll supervise the session tomorrow and tell her what's been going on,' Zoe told me.

'I'll come along too,' I replied. 'Saskia might be more willing to open up if her mum is there.'

I knew when we told Rosa what James had been doing, she was going to be furious.

As always, Saskia was delighted to see her mum and gave her a big hug.

'How's your week been, sweetheart?' Rosa asked her as we all got settled in the contact room.

Saskia shrugged, obviously not wanting to raise anything about what had happened yesterday herself.

'Have the police told you anything about going to prison?' she asked anxiously.

'Not yet,' Rosa told her. 'It will be a magistrate or a judge who decides that, and I'm still waiting for a court date.

'Don't worry,' Rosa added, squeezing Saskia's hand. 'I'll tell you as soon as I hear. It will all work out.'

Saskia nodded.

'Rosa, there's something I wanted to discuss with you,' Zoe piped up. 'Maggie, do you want to tell Rosa what happened yesterday?'

Saskia started nervously fiddling with her hair.

I explained about the dentist's appointment and how I'd gone to pick her up and seen James getting into the car.

'He did what?' Rosa gasped. 'What on earth was he thinking?'

She looked at Saskia.

'What's been going on, sweetheart?' she asked her. 'Why has your dad been getting into the car with you?'

Tears immediately filled Saskia's eyes and I could see she was trying not to cry.

'He shouldn't have done that, Saskia,' Rosa told her firmly. 'He's broken his agreement with Social Services and that wasn't very fair of him.'

Saskia nodded.

'What did he talk to you about in the car, sweetie?' Rosa asked her.

'Nothing much,' shrugged Saskia.

'What, all of those times he and Dave drove you home? You must have talked about something?'

Saskia shrugged.

Rosa edged nearer to her on the sofa.

'Sweetheart, this is very real,' she told her. 'I might go to prison and the way things are going, it's looking very likely that you're going to be going back to live with your dad full time.'

She paused.

'So if you have any worries or concerns, or if there is any reason why you don't want to be with your dad, then this is the time to tell us.'

Saskia looked down at the floor and I could see that she was shaking.

Rosa grabbed her hand.

'Please, Saskie,' she whispered. 'I know there's something bothering you. I knew it before we went to Spain and I know it now. I'm your mama, you can talk to me about anything. Please, just tell me, before it's too late.'

Saskia collapsed into Rosa's arms and sobbed her heart out.

TWELVE

Coming Clean

'Oh, Saskia, it's OK,' soothed Rosa, stroking her long brown hair.

'Talk to me, sweetie,' she begged. 'Please tell me what's been going on.'

'I don't want to go and live with him, Mum,' Saskia sobbed. 'Please don't make me. Please don't leave me there.' She could barely speak for crying and her eyes were full of fear.

'Why haven't you said something before now?' asked Rosa. 'Why didn't you tell Maggie and Zoe this?'

We'd both spent the past few weeks asking her over and over again if going to live with James was what she wanted.

''Cos Dad told me not to,' she wept. 'He said Social Services were going to give me back to him but if I said I didn't want to go, he'd stop me from seeing you forever. I'd be so sad if I was never allowed to see you again.'

My heart ached for Saskia. She'd obviously been walking around with this hanging over her head for the past few weeks.

'Was that what your dad was saying to you when he got in the car after school?' Zoe asked her.

Saskia nodded.

'He was telling me what I had to say to you and Maggie, and I did what he wanted because I wanted to see Mum again.'

'Oh, Saskia,' sighed Rosa. 'I would never let that happen, I would never let him do that and I'd always fight to see you.'

'He said a judge would always believe him and not you,' she sobbed. 'He said he could afford the best lawyers, and you had nothing.'

Rosa had been right about James. What an awful, manipulative man, threatening his own daughter like that.

Saskia turned to Rosa.

'I want to stay with you,' she begged. 'Why can't I come and live with you, Mum?'

I could see Rosa was becoming distressed now.

'I desperately want that too, but at the moment I don't think Social Services will allow that,' Rosa told Saskia, her voice breaking. 'Not before the court case anyway.'

Zoe and I looked at each other – what Rosa was saying was true. Social Services wouldn't want to send Saskia to live with Rosa if she was going to be sent to prison a few months later, as Saskia would have to move again. It would cause a lot more upheaval than her remaining where she was.

'Thank you for being honest with us, Saskia,' Zoe told her. 'Our job is to make sure that you're living somewhere where you're happy and safe.'

'I won't be happy or safe if I have to go and live with him,' she sobbed. 'I hated the weeks when it was Dad's turn to have me.'

'Tell me why was it so awful, sweetheart?' Rosa asked her. 'What happened when you were with your dad?'

Saskia started to cry again.

'I can't,' she sobbed. 'He told me I wasn't allowed to say anything.'

Zoe and I turned to look at each other.

'Saskia, please tell me,' begged Rosa. 'Then we can all make sure that you never have to go back and live there again.'

Saskia nodded.

'It was horrible there,' she said. 'He had his friends round at night and at the weekend and they would drink and take lots of drugs.'

'Drugs?' gasped Rosa.

'Do you know what kind of drugs, Saskia?' asked Zoe calmly.

She shrugged.

'I don't know the names,' she replied. 'White powder that looks like the powder you put in the washing machine, and little blue, pink and yellow tablets in these clear plastic bags. They had hearts, skulls and smiley faces on them, and they looked like sweets.'

'What would you do when your dad and his friends were taking drugs?' I asked her.

'He wanted me out of the way, so he'd make me a hot chocolate and I'd stay in my room, and then go to bed,' she said.

She described how, when she'd get up in the morning, she'd see the white powder on tables, on the kitchen worktops and by the sink in the toilet.

'It was everywhere,' she said. 'There were lots of bags of it in the kitchen drawers and in the bathroom cabinet, and I even found a little bag in my bedside table once.'

Rosa looked absolutely horrified.

'Oh, sweetheart,' she sighed. 'I can't believe you've kept all of this to yourself for so long. Why did you never tell me any of this? When you were at my house, you could have told me and I would have made sure you never went back to him again.'

Tears filled Saskia's eyes.

'I wanted to, Mum, but Dad made me so scared to say anything,' she sighed. 'He said no one would believe you and he would go for full custody, and I'd have to live with him all the time.'

'But, sweetheart, couldn't you have said something to me when we were in Spain?' Rosa asked.

'I didn't need to because I was safe there and I thought we'd never have to see Dad again,' Saskia sobbed. 'Then when the police made us come back here, I was so scared. When they said they were taking me back to Dad's house, I panicked. I was shouting and screaming at them not to leave me there.'

It was Rosa's turn to break down.

'I'm so sorry, Saskia,' she sobbed. 'I should have known. I feel like I've let you down.'

'Don't cry, Mum,' Saskia told her. 'You knew I wasn't happy. That's why you took me to Spain.'

I had a lump in my throat as I watched mum and daughter sob in each other's arms. Everything was starting to make sense and I was relieved that Saskia had opened up to us at last.

Slowly, Saskia's tears stopped and Rosa also started to calm down.

'Saskia, me and Maggie are going to chat to your mum,' Zoe told her. 'Are you OK to stay in here with a contact worker?'

She nodded.

'Will you come back, Mum?' she asked Rosa anxiously.

'Of course I will, sweetheart,' Rosa told her, squeezing her hand. 'It will just be for a few minutes.'

Zoe led us all into an office off reception.

'What an emotional afternoon for you,' Zoe told Rosa. 'It must be a shock to find out how Saskia is really feeling.'

Rosa nodded.

'I feel so guilty,' she said. 'I've let my daughter down. I knew she wasn't happy and that there was something happening at home with James, but I should have pushed her more and asked more questions.'

'It's not your fault,' I told her gently. 'We've been trying to get Saskia to open up to us too. We can all see what a manipulative man he is. He obviously put the fear of God into Saskia and she was too terrified to say anything to any of us.'

'I know,' sighed Rosa. 'But I'll always blame myself. A child shouldn't be living in an environment where grown men are taking drugs and they're left littered all around the house.'

'Are you surprised about the drugs?' Zoe asked her. 'Did you know James took them?'

'I'm disgusted but not surprised,' Rosa replied. 'I knew James occasionally took cocaine recreationally and we fell out over it a few times, but it was always on nights out – never, ever at home. I would never have allowed it, not around Saskia, but it looks like his habit has escalated.'

She shook her head. 'I'm so angry with him. How dare he put my daughter at risk like that while making me out to be a terrible mother?

'What happens now?' she asked. 'I don't want that man going anywhere near my daughter ever again.'

'That's a good question,' I said, looking at Zoe.

'Surely Social Services won't send her to live with a man who has a drug problem?' said Rosa. 'I don't want him having any contact with her at all.'

It was a Friday afternoon so James's next contact session with Saskia wasn't until early the following week.

'Firstly, I'm going to talk to my manager – I assume that he'll want us to call the police,' Zoe said. 'They're probably going to want Saskia to make a statement at some stage.'

'And what about James?' asked Rosa. 'Are you going to tell him what Saskia has told us?'

I could see Zoe was mulling it over.

'Let me talk to my manager,' she replied. 'We'll definitely need to tell him we're putting contact on hold for now, but the police probably won't want us to alert him as to why.'

I assumed the police would want to search his house and we didn't want to risk James destroying any evidence.

'I'll keep everyone posted with any developments,' Zoe told us.

'Thank you,' Rosa replied.

Saskia looked relieved to see Rosa walk back into the room. Rosa sat down next to Saskia and tenderly stroked her daughter's cheek.

'Are you feeling better now, my love?' she asked her and Saskia nodded.

'I'm really sorry but I'm afraid we're going to have to wrap up this session now as the room's booked for another family,' said Zoe.

Saskia looked panicked.

'When will I see you again?' she asked Rosa. 'Will I still have to see my dad?'

'Contact with your mum will carry on as normal,' Zoe told her. 'But we'll pause the sessions with your dad for now.'

'They're going to report him to the police,' Rosa said.

'Saskia, as you know, possessing and taking certain drugs is illegal so the police will want to speak to him and they might want to speak to you too,' Zoe told her.

Saskia nodded.

'Don't you worry, it's going to be OK,' Rosa reassured her.

They both became very tearful again as they said goodbye.

'I'm so sorry for letting you down, Saskia,' Rosa told her as she gave her a hug.

'You haven't, Mum,' she said.

Saskia was very quiet in the car on the way home from the contact centre.

'You've been so brave today,' I told her. 'It must have been really hard for you to tell us those things about your dad.'

'I'm sorry, Maggie,' she said sheepishly. 'Are you and Zoe cross at me for not telling you the truth?'

'Not at all,' I told her. 'The only thing I'm cross about is that your dad made you so scared that you didn't feel like you could tell anyone the truth, but I'm so glad you did. It must have been horrible for you living like that.'

'It was,' she said. 'I hated it.'

As soon as we walked through the door, Saskia went up to her bedroom. She looked exhausted and I knew she probably needed some time just to digest everything that had happened that afternoon.

When my mobile rang, I leapt to answer it, thinking it might be Zoe.

It was Louisa.

'I wondered if you and Saskia wanted to meet me and Edie at the park tomorrow?' she asked.

'That would have been lovely, flower, but there's quite a lot going on here at the minute and I might have to go to the police station tomorrow.'

'Police?' gasped Louisa. 'What's happened? Is it PJ again?' she said, sounding panicked.

'No, it's not to do with him,' I told her. 'It's something to do with Saskia.'

'Well, I hope everything's OK?' she asked me.

'I think it will be,' I said.

We arranged to speak again over the weekend and I got on with making dinner, all the while checking my phone for any updates from Zoe.

She called me just after 6 p.m.

'I had a chat to Brian, and I've called the police,' she told me. She said they were going to arrest James on suspicion of possession of Class A drugs and obtain a warrant to search his house.

'Because of what Saskia told us about the amount of drugs in the house and people coming round, they suspect James might also have been dealing,' she added.

Zoe had also let James know that his contact sessions with Saskia were on hold for the time being. 'I told him that Social Services were reviewing things because we found out that he'd been getting into Saskia's car after school.'

'How did he take that?' I asked.

'He put the phone down on me,' she replied. 'But just before that, he'd had the audacity to claim that Saskia had begged to see him and asked him to be in the car on her way home from school! The arrogance of that man is unbelievable.'

'He clearly doesn't seem to care about the needs or welfare of his daughter,' I nodded.

He'd already got his lawyer on the case.

'Since then, Brian and I have had his lawyer on the phone multiple times already, threatening us with all sorts and demanding that we reinstate contact immediately,' Zoe said.

Saskia spent the rest of the evening in her room and I didn't push her to come down. I gave Vicky a quick call as I felt I needed a chat.

'Is everything OK?' she asked.

I explained what had happened that afternoon.

'At least now you know what's been going on,' she said.

'That's true,' I replied. 'But where does all this leave Saskia?'

Now both of her parents were potentially going to court and facing prison.

'I really feel for her,' I sighed. 'She's been through such a lot and now this on top of it all.'

As the following day was Saturday, Saskia and I had a quiet one at home. I wanted to try to do something with Saskia to help relax her and distract her from everything else that was going on.

'Come downstairs,' I told her when I went up to her bedroom. 'I'm going to teach you how to knit.'

'Knit?' she laughed, and I realised it was the first time that I'd seen her smile in a few days.

'Yes,' I nodded. 'It will be fun.'

'OK,' she sighed.

I always found knitting or sewing or any kind of crafting was therapeutic for children when there were difficult things going on in their lives. Knitting was something I liked to do from time to time, and I found it really relaxing. I'd already got out the wool and the knitting needles, and I showed Saskia how to cast on.

'I don't think I'm going to be any good at this,' she sighed.

'That doesn't matter,' I told her. 'Just give it a go.'

Soon she'd managed to knit a whole line.

'Perhaps you could make something to give to your mum?' I said.

'I could make her a blanket,' Saskia suggested. 'Then she could take it with her if she goes to prison.'

Suddenly I saw the sadness creep back into her eyes.

'Saskia, whatever happens, it will be OK,' I told her. 'You and your mum will get through it.'

She nodded.

'I know things probably feel really scary and overwhelming at the minute but I'm here to support you through it,' I added.

'I know,' she said, head down focusing on her knitting.

'You're doing really well,' I smiled. 'You're going to have a cosy blanket for your mum in no time.'

I wasn't quite sure how much she was enjoying it but for the next hour, we sat side by side doing our knitting and I felt that it had helped to calm Saskia's mind a little.

That afternoon, while Saskia caught up on some homework, I decided to do some cleaning. I'd been vacuuming the living room when I walked back into the kitchen and glanced at my phone.

There was a missed call from Zoe. She'd left a voicemail.

'Maggie, sorry to bother you on a Saturday but please can you ring me urgently,' she said. 'It's about James.'

It was unusual to get a call from a social worker at the weekend but I knew that the police were due to arrest James today.

I called her back straight away.

'Sorry I missed you,' I told her. 'I was doing some vacuuming and I didn't hear my phone. Is everything OK?'

'Not really,' she said. 'The police searched James's house today.'

'What did they find? Has he been dealing drugs like they suspected?'

'No, it's not to do with drugs,' she told me. 'They found something else. Something on his phone.'

I could tell by the tone of her voice that it wasn't good.

'What is it, Zoe?' I asked. 'Please tell me.'

What she said next completely floored me.

'They found some photos, Maggie . . . explicit photos.'

She paused.

'The police said they're of Saskia.'

THIRTEEN

Secrecy and Shock

We've all experienced those rare moments when you're in such a state of shock that you struggle to get any words out. That's exactly how I felt as Zoe explained what had happened.

I couldn't believe what I was hearing.

'Explicit photos?' I gasped. 'Surely it's not Saskia in them? The police must have made a mistake?'

It was sickening that James had these indecent images in the first place, but were they really of his own daughter? It was just too horrific to contemplate.

'I'm afraid it looks like it's true, Maggie,' replied Zoe. 'I'm as disgusted as you are but the police are pretty certain.'

I felt sick to my stomach as she described how they'd found around ten indecent photographs of Saskia on James's phone.

'The police said you can't really see her face in them but she's lying on her bed and her pyjama top is pulled up and her bottoms are pulled down and . . .'

'Please stop,' I interrupted. 'I don't think I can bear to hear any more.'

'I know,' sighed Zoe. 'It's just awful that anyone would do that to a child, and their own child too.'

She explained that CID had a special unit that dealt with this kind of crime and that they had been analysing the photos, as well as going through James's other devices that had since been seized. From what they'd seen so far, he didn't appear to have sent or circulated the images to anyone else, which was one small mercy.

'But how do they know it's definitely Saskia if they can't see her face?' I asked.

She told me the police had matched the background to Saskia's bedroom and they'd found both pairs of pyjamas featured in the photographs in the drawers at the house. The location on James's phone had been switched on, which also confirmed the photos had been taken in the house.

'In the photos, you can also see a scar on the child's left knee and it fits Saskia's medical records that say she had to go to hospital to get her knee stitched when she was nine,' Zoe told me.

It was just utterly horrific.

Zoe explained the photos were taken in the six months before Saskia went to Spain, on three separate occasions.

'No wonder she didn't want to come back and live with her dad,' I sighed. 'Poor Saskia.'

'Why didn't she confide in us?' I continued. 'She could have told us about it the other day when she told us about the drugs.'

'Perhaps she's blocked it out in her own mind or it's just too traumatic for her?' suggested Zoe. 'She probably feels a lot of shame and fear as well.'

'Or maybe she doesn't want Rosa to know?' I added. 'Assuming that she doesn't know.'

I couldn't imagine that if Rosa had known James had done such a disturbing thing to their daughter, she would have kept it to herself.

'Fancy lawyers or not, surely she would have gone straight to the police if she'd found out about the photos?'

'We'll have to find all of this out in time,' Zoe told me. 'I'm sorry to break such awful news to you over the phone – I just felt like you needed to know as soon as possible.'

'It's OK,' I sighed. 'There's no good way to find out something like this.'

It was truly shocking and my head was spinning.

'What on earth happens now?' I asked Zoe.

Did I come off the phone and pretend everything was normal to Saskia when I knew that she'd been through the most sickening ordeal at the hands of her own father?

'I know it's hard, Maggie, but please don't say anything to Saskia until we know more,' said Zoe. 'The police want to question her and they don't want anyone talking to her about it first.'

'I understand,' I told her.

Carers always had to be really careful when children were giving a statement to police. We didn't want to be accused of influencing them in any way or be seen to have spoken to them about it. I didn't want to do anything that risked that statement not being able to be used in any future court case. I would never forgive myself if a trial collapsed because I hadn't followed the correct guidance.

'They've assured me they have specially trained officers who will question her,' Zoe added. 'They also want to question

Rosa as well, before anyone else breaks the news to her and she speaks to Saskia.'

Poor Rosa.

'She's going to be beside herself when she knows what Saskia's been through,' I sighed.

Zoe also explained that the police wanted more time to search James's other devices.

'I'm afraid that in all likelihood it's going to be Monday morning before they question her,' Zoe told me.

'OK,' I sighed.

I knew there was nothing I could do. An almost entire weekend felt a long time to keep up the pretence with Saskia, but I knew it was for the best in the long term.

'We'll need to let her school know that Saskia won't be in on Monday morning,' said Zoe.

'What will I tell her about why she's going to the police station?' I panicked.

'Just say the police wanted to ask her some questions about her dad and the drugs,' Zoe told me. 'We already told her that they'd probably want to speak to her about that.'

'I'll see you at the police station on Monday morning and I'll message you tomorrow to confirm everything,' she added. 'I know it will be hard for you to keep this from her, Maggie, but it's in Saskia's best interests.'

'I know,' I sighed.

It didn't make it any easier though.

As I put the phone down, I felt shell-shocked. I made myself a strong cup of sweet tea to help calm my nerves. It was a chilly November afternoon and already getting dark, but I put my big coat on and went out into the garden. I took some deep, gulping breaths of cold winter air and tried to get my head around what I'd just been told.

I had so many questions – had James done this before? Why hadn't Saskia told anyone? – but I knew they would all have to wait until Monday.

I sipped my tea and stared at my messy garden. Saskia was still upstairs doing her homework, and I needed to take a breath before I went inside and pretended that everything was normal. Being a foster carer, I was used to having to withhold certain information from children, but this felt particularly hard. I just hoped Saskia would be OK, and that she would be able to cope with talking about this horrible trauma.

Over the past few weeks, I had seen glimpses of what Saskia could be: a happy, carefree child when she was with the people who loved her. She was diligent at school and was a delight to be around. Her outlook on life, considering all that had happened to her, was remarkable, and I knew she still held on to the hope of being fully reunited with her mum.

After I'd taken my last gulp of tea, I went back inside and headed upstairs to see Saskia. As I pushed open her bedroom door, I took a deep breath and swallowed the nervous lump in my throat.

'All OK, lovey?' I asked her, keeping my voice casual.

'Yes,' she nodded. 'I'm just doing some maths. It's so boring.'

'Good girl,' I smiled. 'Dinner will be in an hour.'

I knew the pretence was for Saskia's own good but every time I looked at her, I felt like bursting into tears.

However, I did my best to keep everything as normal as possible. That night, we had dinner and then watched a film together. But as I stared at the TV, I wasn't really paying any attention. I was thinking about Saskia and my heart was aching at what she'd been through and what was to come.

On Sunday afternoon, I suggested that we paint some stones together.

'I sometimes do this with Edie and she loves it,' I told Saskia.

'OK,' she sighed.

I painted one stone like a ladybird while Saskia did a bumblebee.

'Maybe we could hide them in the garden when they're dry, then Edie can find them the next time she comes round?' she suggested.

'That's a lovely idea,' I smiled. 'She'd really like that.'

I could see Saskia deep in thought. 'I think I can remember doing this with stones with my mum when I was little,' she told me.

'Did you do a lot of crafts with your mum?' I asked her.

'Yep,' she nodded. 'Mum's really good at art. She can paint pictures too.'

As we sat at the kitchen table and did our painting, I knew I had to somehow let Saskia know about the police.

'Oh, by the way, the police want to talk to you again,' I told her.

'Why?' she asked, looking pensive.

'I think they've got some questions about your dad,' I told her. 'You know, about the drugs and things. They want you to make a statement. I'll take you to the police station tomorrow morning.'

'The same one?' she asked, and I nodded.

She seemed to take it OK, and we got on with our painting.

Thankfully Saskia seemed fine, but that night I hardly slept a wink. I spent the whole time tossing and turning and going over everything again and again in my mind. I felt sick at the thought of the police confronting Saskia with what they'd found and I wasn't sure how she was going to react to the fact that we all knew.

The following morning, we got in the car and headed to the police headquarters.

Saskia had been very quiet over breakfast.

'Shall I put my uniform on?' she'd asked me. 'I know you're probably going to make me go to school after the police station.'

I didn't think she'd be in any fit state to go back to school after the questions the police were going to ask her, but I didn't want to say that and worry her.

'No, I think just go in normal clothes for now,' I'd said. 'We'll put your uniform and school bag in the car just in case.'

I didn't want to arouse too much suspicion, but Saskia had looked surprised.

'OK, lovey?' I asked now, looking at her in the rear-view mirror.

'Yep,' she shrugged. 'Though I don't like going here and I'm fed up of people asking me questions.'

I suppose the building held bad memories for her, of when she and Rosa had first returned from Spain and Rosa had been arrested and held.

Zoe was waiting for us in reception.

'Morning, Maggie,' she said. 'Everything OK?'

We both exchanged knowing looks.

'Yes,' I nodded. 'I think so.'

My stomach was churning with dread in anticipation of what was to come.

'Do you know who we need to ask for?' I said to Zoe.

'Oh, are we seeing different police officers this time?' asked Saskia curiously.

'Yes, lovey,' I replied. 'It's probably going to be in a different area of the police station today as well.'

Zoe had already told me they were going to take Saskia to what was called a video interview suite, where children who had been victims of sexual offences were questioned. I'd sadly been in a few of these in my years of fostering and they were either part of a police station, a hospital or in a completely separate building. They usually consisted of a family room or communal area with sofas and toys and a kitchen, an examination room and an interview room. Police stations tended to be busy and intimidating places, and these other types of areas provided a safe haven away from that and were designed to make children feel more relaxed.

Saskia looked apprehensive as the automatic door next to the reception desk suddenly buzzed open and two women came out and walked towards us. One had long dark hair and looked to be in her early forties, and the other had bobbed blonde hair. They both looked approachable and friendly, and I was thankful that it looked like Saskia would be in good hands for this.

'I'm DC Lizzie Bangs,' the dark-haired woman said, holding out her hand to Zoe.

Zoe introduced me and then Saskia.

'Hi, Saskia,' Lizzie smiled. 'Me and my colleague DC Amy Wellbeck are going to be chatting to you today.'

'You're not wearing a uniform?' she said to Lizzie curiously.

'No, that's right,' smiled Lizzie. 'Amy and I are DCs, which stands for Detective Constable, and we work for CID so we don't wear uniforms.'

Saskia nodded and Amy gave her a little smile.

'Shall we go through, and I'll show you where we'll be chatting today,' Amy told her.

We followed them down a corridor and through some double doors. Eventually we came to a security door and Lizzie tapped her pass on the entrance pad. The door opened and we walked into a large room. Everything looked brand new and was bright and clean. The walls were painted a soft blue and there were two big green sofas and a table and chairs. There were also some boxes of toys and books, and an area to make tea and coffee and other drinks.

'This is loads nicer than where me and Mum were last time,' said Saskia, looking around.

'This is our family room,' smiled Lizzie. 'I can get you a drink if you'd like one?'

'I'm OK,' smiled Saskia.

Then they led us into another room.

'This is our interview room where Lizzie and I are going to ask you some questions,' explained Amy. 'And see those things on the walls?'

Saskia nodded.

'They're cameras,' she told her. 'And when we ask you questions, those cameras are going to film it.'

'Why do you want to video me?' asked Saskia.

'That's a good question,' nodded Amy. 'We want to talk to you about your dad, and if he eventually has to go to court then your video can be shown to the court and used as evidence.'

At the mention of court, Saskia looked worried and confused.

'Maggie and Zoe can stay if you like?' Lizzie suggested.

Saskia nodded.

Neither Zoe nor I were potential witnesses in the case, so we were able to sit in on her interview. We weren't allowed to sit alongside Saskia, in case we were accused of coercion or putting words into Saskia's mouth, but there were two chairs at the back of the room from where we could observe.

First of all, the police asked Saskia about James and his drug use, including what she'd seen at the house and how often it had happened. Even though I could tell she was nervous, Saskia answered their questions clearly and told them exactly what she'd told Zoe and me the other day. I was proud of how grown up she was being and how seriously she was treating their questions.

'When your dad was arrested on Saturday, the police took his phone and his laptop off him,' explained Lizzie. 'They wanted to look at his messages and emails to try and get some idea of where he might have been getting his drugs from.'

Lizzie paused. I held my breath as I knew we were getting to the difficult part.

'When they were looking at his devices, they came across some photographs of you. Did your dad used to take photos of you?' she asked.

'Sometimes,' shrugged Saskia.

'When would he take photos of you?' asked Lizzie.

'On holiday sometimes, at Christmas and birthdays and stuff,' she replied. 'But it was my mum who took most of the photos.'

Lizzie looked down at her notes.

'Saskia, when the police looked at your dad's phone, they found some photos of you on it.'

She looked puzzled.

'He probably has lots of photos of me,' she replied.

By now, my heart was pounding out of my chest.

'These were what we'd call explicit photos,' Lizzie explained gently. 'Do you know what that means?'

Saskia shook her head.

'The photos were of you in your bedroom,' she continued. 'You're lying on your bed and in some of the images your pyjama top is pulled up so you can see your breasts. In others, your pyjama bottoms are pulled down so you can see your private parts, and sometimes, in other images, your bottom.'

Saskia went bright red. She looked horrified.

'But that's not true,' she gasped. 'Why are you saying those things? That's disgusting! Why would my dad have photos like that?'

'Saskia, we found these photos of you on your dad's phone,' said Lizzie. 'Can you tell us when he might have taken them?'

'You're lying!' yelled Saskia, close to tears by now. 'Dad didn't take those photos! I wouldn't let him!'

She looked mortified.

'Saskia, we know how frightened you were of your dad and how he manipulated you,' Amy told her gently. 'I know you're probably very scared right now but I promise you, you won't get into trouble for talking to us about this.'

Saskia shook her head.

'But he didn't take any photos,' she said, clearly still upset. 'I'd tell you if he had. Why are you making things up? I swear it's not me.'

She was crying now.

'Saskia, I can see you're upset so I'm going to ask you one last time,' said Lizzie slowly. 'I don't want you to be scared or worried or ashamed. This is not your fault and you won't get into trouble but we need to know the truth. Did your dad take these photos of you?'

Tears streamed down Saskia's face.

'No,' she sobbed. 'I already told you he didn't take any photos. I promise I'm telling the truth.'

She turned round and looked at me. She seemed genuinely shocked.

'Maggie, tell them it's not true,' she said. 'Why won't they believe me?'

I couldn't intervene in the interview, so could only look on with compassion.

'I'm going to show you some of the photos that we found,' Amy told her.

'No, I don't want to see them!' Saskia cried.

'We've zoomed in on certain parts of them,' Amy reassured her. 'We're not going to show you anything upsetting.'

She got out a bundle of images from a folder.

'Do you recognise those certificates?' Amy asked her.

'They're my gymnastic certificates from when I was little,' Saskia nodded. 'I have them up on my bedroom wall.'

Amy showed her another zoomed-in image.

'Do you recognise those?' she asked her.

'They're my lemon pyjamas that Mum got me for Christmas,' replied Saskia.

'There's also another pair in one of the photos with unicorns on,' said Amy. 'And we found those in a drawer at your dad's house so we know that they're your pyjamas.'

'They might be the same pyjamas but it's not me,' said Saskia firmly. 'Why are you making these disgusting things up?'

I felt so sorry for her.

'Saskia, have you got any scars?' Amy asked her.

Saskia nodded.

'I fell over on my bike when I was little and landed on some glass,' she replied. 'I had to go to hospital and have stitches.'

'And where were your stitches?' asked Amy.

'On my knee,' nodded Saskia. 'This one,' she said, tapping her left knee.

Amy showed her another zoomed-in image.

'Saskia, the girl in all of these photos has a little scar on her left knee exactly where you've just told us.'

She pointed to the scar on the photo. Saskia's face crumpled.

'I don't understand,' she sobbed. 'It can't be me.'

Now Lizzie took over.

'Saskia, I know it must be so upsetting for you, but we need you to talk to us about these photos so we can make sure your dad never does anything like this ever again,' Lizzie told her. 'Please don't be scared to tell us the truth – you're not going to get in any trouble.'

Saskia was weeping now.

'I *am* telling you the truth,' she said. 'I really am. If I remembered then I'd tell you but I don't. I swear I don't remember my dad taking those photos of me.'

Zoe and I looked at each other. I could tell from the expression on her face that we'd both had the same horrible realisation.

FOURTEEN

The Unknown

By now, Saskia was becoming more and more upset. I knew I was there as an observer and I couldn't interrupt a police interview, so it was a relief when Lizzie stepped in.

'Why don't we pause things there and have a quick break?' she suggested.

'I think that's a good idea,' nodded Amy.

'Maggie and I could go and get everyone a drink?' Zoe suggested.

My priority was to comfort Saskia, who was in a huge amount of distress. I went over to her and gave her a hug.

'I know this is so hard for you, but you're doing really well,' I soothed.

'I swear I'm telling the truth, Maggie,' she told me. 'Those are my pyjamas and that's my bedroom, but I don't remember Dad taking any photos of me. I'd tell them if he had 'cos that's disgusting.'

'I know, flower,' I told her. 'You're doing really well.' I handed her a tissue from my bag while my thoughts jumbled together.

There was another possibility that I was churning over in my mind and I knew I needed to talk it through with the police officers first.

'I'm just going to nip out briefly to the other room and help Zoe with the drinks,' I told her. 'Shall I get you a water or a squash?'

'Yes, a squash, please,' Saskia replied.

Zoe was boiling the kettle in the family room.

'That was really hard to watch,' she sighed. 'Do you think she's telling the truth?'

'I really do think she is. She's got no reason to lie.'

'Maybe she genuinely doesn't remember?' suggested Zoe. 'Like we said earlier, perhaps it was so traumatic for her that she's just blocked it all out?'

'It could be that,' I replied.

Sadly, I'd come across young people in the past who had what was referred to as dissociative amnesia. Some doctors believe that certain events, such as sexual abuse, are so overwhelming and traumatic that the brain blocks them out and the child can't access those memories. Sometimes they resurfaced in adulthood, or with the help of counselling or therapy.

Lizzie came out to join us.

'Amy's staying with Saskia,' she told us. 'She seems to be calming down a little bit.'

'I don't know what your feeling is, but I genuinely believe that Saskia knows nothing about those photographs,' I said to her.

'What does she look like in the photos?' asked Zoe. 'Could it be that they were taken when she was asleep, which is why she's got no recollection of them?'

I didn't want to ask to see them as I knew I would find it too upsetting.

'Her head is turned to one side in a few of the images and in others you can see that her eyes are closed,' nodded Lizzie. 'When CID analysed them, they said she looked like she was either asleep or perhaps pretending to be asleep, as some children do that to get through such an ordeal. Or perhaps James made her do that for the photo?'

In my mind, there was another explanation.

'Could it be possible that James was drugging Saskia?' I asked.

Lizzie nodded.

'After what Saskia has told us today, that's definitely one possibility that we need to look at,' she replied. 'I'd had the same thought.'

She explained that as well as cocaine, a large amount of ketamine had been found at the house.

'As you might know, ketamine can be used as an anaesthetic to put people and even animals to sleep before surgery,' said Lizzie.

'I'm sure Saskia mentioned that James made her a hot chocolate before bed when his friends were round,' added Zoe.

'But if James had drugged her, how could you prove it?' I asked.

'Sadly, it's unlikely to show up in any blood tests now,' Lizzie told us.

The photographs had been taken over six months ago and she explained that ketamine only showed up in blood tests for a few weeks at the very maximum.

As we were all talking, another thought entered my mind. A thought so terrible that I didn't want to say it out loud but I felt that somebody needed to voice it.

'If James did drug Saskia, then what else might he and possibly his friends have done to her?' I asked. 'What if it's not just photographs? What if he abused her too?'

'This is the worry,' sighed Lizzie. 'One option we do have is having a doctor examine Saskia to see if there are signs that any sexual abuse has taken place, but we'd need Rosa's consent, and Saskia's too, of course.'

At thirteen, she was old enough to understand and decide whether she wanted to have such an invasive examination.

This situation was getting more and more shocking by the minute.

'What do we tell Saskia?' asked Zoe.

'The truth,' I said, and Lizzie nodded.

'It's horrific, but she needs to know,' she agreed.

We went back in with the drinks. Lizzie was right, Saskia seemed a bit calmer. However, I knew that after what was coming, it wouldn't be for long.

After we'd finished our drinks, Lizzie told Saskia that she was going to resume the interview and put the cameras back on.

'Saskia, if you don't remember your dad taking the photos, then there could be one other possibility,' she suggested.

She gently explained about the ketamine.

'If your dad had given you some ketamine then it effectively would mean that you were unconscious,' she explained.

Saskia's face fell.

'But I don't understand,' she questioned. 'Why would he give me drugs? Why would he do that to me?'

'Your dad might have wanted you to be asleep so that you wouldn't know what he was doing,' Lizzie told her.

I felt sick to my stomach. It was all so hard to explain to a child.

I could see Saskia was struggling to take it all in as Lizzie asked her more questions. She confirmed that her dad normally made her a hot chocolate before she went to bed when his friends were around.

'Did you feel any different when you woke up in the morning?' Amy asked her. 'Were you very groggy or did you feel any pain anywhere?'

'I don't remember,' she said. 'It was so long ago.'

Then they had to drop the biggest bombshell.

'Saskia, we also need to look at the possibility that, if you were drugged, your dad or some other individuals might have sexually abused you,' Amy told her gently.

Saskia looked stunned.

'No!' she cried, shaking her head. 'No, he wouldn't do that to me, would he?'

'I know it must be so hard for you to think about, but I'm afraid we do have to look at all the possibilities,' Lizzie told her. 'That could also be why your dad gave you the drugs.'

Saskia was getting very tearful again.

'You're lying,' she sobbed. 'That's not right. You're making things up now. Please shut up.'

She was becoming more and more anguished. I knew I couldn't interrupt the interview but Zoe and I looked anxiously at each other.

'Saskia, I can see how upset you are, so I think we'll stop things there for today,' Lizzie told her.

I was extremely relieved as by now Saskia was sobbing her heart out. I walked over to her and put my arms around her.

'It's OK,' I soothed. 'I know it's a lot for you to take in. You've been so brave.'

I held her in my arms as her body shook with sobs.

'I swear I didn't know,' she cried. 'I didn't know about the pictures or any of it.'

'Lovey, if he drugged you then you wouldn't have known,' I told her gently.

'But what else might he have done to me?' she wept. 'What if the police are right?'

'I know it's so hard to comprehend, but we'll try to get some answers,' I told her. 'We'll talk about all that later.'

Saskia let out a deep, gulping sob.

'I want my mum,' she whimpered. 'Please can I see her?'

I looked at Zoe. It wasn't a day that Rosa was due to have contact.

'The police need to speak to your mum first,' she told her. 'But perhaps we could all meet at Social Services after she's been interviewed?'

'Are they going to tell her what he did to me?' she asked.

'Yes,' I nodded. 'They have to, as they'll want to see if she knows anything.'

'How could she know?' sobbed Saskia. 'I didn't know. How could she?'

I knew how devastated Rosa was going to be to learn what James had put their daughter through.

Saskia went to the toilet, so Zoe and I had time for a quick catch up.

'I'm going to take her back to my house now,' I told her.

'I hope she's OK,' she nodded. 'Let's not worry about school today or tomorrow either.'

Zoe said she was going to stay at the police station to see Rosa.

'I'll talk to her after she's been interviewed and then bring her to Social Services, assuming that she wants to see Saskia?'

'I'm sure she will,' I sighed. 'They're both going to be in bits.'

It was such a horrific thing to get their heads around.

Saskia was still very tearful on the drive home. I could see she was still in shock and I didn't push her to talk.

'Could you manage something to eat?' I asked her when we got back, but she shook her head.

'I'm going to go and lie down,' she said. 'My head hurts.'

I knew that she probably needed some space and time on her own to try to start to process what she'd just been told.

While Saskia was in her bedroom, I called my supervising social worker, Becky, and filled her in on what had happened.

'Oh, Maggie,' she sighed. 'That's horrendous. How's Saskia taking it?'

'She's in shock and very tearful,' I told her.

'Which is completely understandable given the circumstances,' replied Becky.

'I never liked the man but I never ever suspected him of anything like this,' I told her. 'It beggars belief how anyone could do that to their own child.'

'It's truly horrific,' agreed Becky.

When I came off the phone, I went to check on Saskia. She was curled up on top of the bed, fast asleep.

I knew she was exhausted, so I left her to nap and I turned to my own therapy – cleaning. I scrubbed and I mopped and I polished, but nothing took away the sense of shock and distress that I'd felt all morning in the pit of my stomach.

*

An hour or so later, my phone rang. It was Zoe.

'How did Rosa take it?' I asked.

'Like Saskia,' she sighed. 'She's in total and utter disbelief.'

She explained that when the police had first told Rosa, she'd been physically sick.

'It's horrendous,' she sighed. 'She's torturing herself and feels as if it's her fault.'

'Does she want to see Saskia?' I asked.

'Yes,' Zoe told me. 'She really does. I'm going to drive her over to Social Services.'

I explained that Saskia was asleep. 'But she's had over an hour and I know she'll want to see her mum, so I'll wake her up now,' I told her.

I went up to Saskia's bedroom and, as I walked in, I could see she was starting to stir.

'How are you doing?' I asked her gently, smoothing down her hair.

She shrugged.

'I don't know,' she sighed. 'I can't make sense of anything – my head's too full.'

'What if he did hurt me when I was asleep, Maggie?' she asked.

'Then we will deal with it,' I told her. 'Your mum, Zoe and I are all here to support you and we will get you through this.'

'Do you still want to see your mum?' I asked her and she nodded.

'We can go to Social Services now and meet her,' I said. 'She and Zoe are on their way there shortly.'

Saskia went to give her face a quick wash and I made her a sandwich to take in the car. Again, she was very quiet. She didn't eat and just stared out of the window.

Zoe had booked a meeting room for us but, as we walked in, Saskia said she needed the loo.

'I'll wait in here for you, lovey,' I told her.

A few minutes later, Zoe and Rosa walked into the meeting room.

Rosa looked deathly pale, and her eyes were puffy and bloodshot from crying.

'Where's Saskie?' she asked, wringing her hands.

'She's just in the loo but she'll be back soon,' I told her. 'How are you doing?'

'It's all my fault,' she sighed. 'I should have got her out of that house sooner.'

As she dabbed her eyes with a tissue, I could see her hands were shaking. 'I should have taken her to Spain as soon as the judge gave us fifty-fifty custody.'

'You weren't to know about James,' I told her.

'But I'm her mother,' she sighed. 'It's my job to protect her and I failed. What was he thinking giving her drugs? He could have killed her.'

Zoe reiterated that we didn't know that for sure.

'I'm convinced that that's what he did,' nodded Rosa. 'It's the only explanation as to why Saskia wouldn't remember anything.'

'How could he have done that to her?' she sniffled. 'His own daughter. My poor baby.'

She looked broken.

Suddenly, there was a voice outside the meeting room.

'Mum? Is that you?'

Saskia walked through the door. Rosa dropped her handbag and ran to her. Saskia burst into tears as she collapsed into her mum's arms.

'Why did he do that to me, Mum?' she sobbed. 'I don't understand.'

Rosa started to cry too as she kissed the top of Saskia's head.

'I don't know, sweetheart,' she told her. 'But I'm so, so sorry. This is all my fault. Please forgive me for leaving you with that monster.'

'But you didn't know, Mum,' Saskia told her. 'None of us did.'

'But I'll never forgive myself,' Rosa wept. 'I wasn't there to protect you.'

I could see her shaking.

'I promise you one thing, Saskia. I'll never let him come near you ever again.'

FIFTEEN

Aftermath

Zoe and I watched as Rosa and Saskia clung on to each other and wept. I could feel the genuine love and empathy between them, and it was clear that a hug from her mum was exactly what Saskia had needed.

'Do you think it's OK to leave them for a while, so they can spend a bit of time together?' I asked Zoe quietly.

I thought they'd appreciate a few moments alone so they could talk and cry and do whatever they needed to do to comfort each other after the day's traumatic events.

Technically, Rosa was still seen as a risk due to her facing charges of child abduction, so she had to be supervised at all times during contact.

'I think that's fine,' nodded Zoe. 'We can sit in reception.'

Rosa and Saskia were sitting down together now.

'I'm happy to leave you together for half an hour while Maggie and I have a chat outside,' said Zoe. 'But give us a shout if you need anything.'

'We will,' Rosa nodded. 'Thank you.'

Despite the upset, I could see how grateful she was to have this time alone with her daughter.

As I sat down on the sofa in reception, I let out a huge breath.

'That was a big sigh,' commented Zoe.

'It's been one heck of a day,' I said.

'It certainly has,' she agreed.

If Zoe and I were struggling to take in everything that had happened, I couldn't imagine how Saskia and Rosa were going to be able to come to terms with it.

'Where do we go from here?' I asked her. 'How can I help Saskia come to terms with something that she doesn't even remember?'

'Maybe, in some strange way, it's a good thing that she doesn't remember James doing anything to her,' said Zoe.

In my mind, there was nothing good about any of this. It was all just horrific and incomprehensible.

'So what happens now?' I asked.

'It all depends on the courts,' replied Zoe. 'Rosa can't offer Saskia a permanent home as we don't know what's going to happen with her court case.'

'And if Rosa gets a custodial sentence?' I asked.

'Then we look at other options,' nodded Zoe. She paused.

'Would you consider having Saskia to stay long term?' she asked. 'Obviously we can't make definite plans until we know if Rosa's going to get a prison sentence and how long that's going to be.'

'Of course,' I smiled. 'I've grown really fond of Saskia. I hate to see her hurting so much and I just want to support her as best I can. If she's happy, then I'm more than happy to have her for as long as she needs me.'

'Thanks, Maggie,' smiled Zoe.

Around fifteen minutes later, Saskia stuck her head out of the meeting room. She looked a lot calmer now and had stopped crying. 'Can I go to the loo?'

'Course you can, darling,' said Zoe, reminding her where the toilets were.

Zoe and I went in to see Rosa. She looked exhausted.

'I still can't believe that he drugged her,' she sighed, squeezing a tissue in her hands. 'He could have killed her.'

'Remember, we don't know that for sure – it's just a theory at this stage,' Zoe told her.

'I'm convinced of it,' said Rosa. 'I know what a light sleeper Saskia is. There's no way James would have been able to adjust her duvet and pull her clothes up and down without waking her. I hope the police lock him up and throw away the key.'

I could see that her distress had now turned to anger.

Zoe talked her through things. 'There's an opportunity for Saskia to be examined by a police doctor, to determine if penetration has taken place,' she explained gently.

Rosa looked like she was going to be sick.

'The police have already mentioned that to me,' she nodded. 'And I just spoke to Saskia about it. As much as I don't want to put her through that, Saskia says she wants to do it.'

I was so proud of Saskia for deciding on this next step. I was hopeful it would help the police with any case they would bring.

'That's very brave of her,' said Zoe. 'If she's sure then let me talk to the police about it.'

Rosa asked if she could be with her for the examination.

'I don't see why not,' said Zoe. 'Maggie could take her and meet you there.'

I nodded.

'Maybe if she gets some answers, then she'll stop torturing herself with the "what ifs",' said Rosa.

I wasn't sure that she was going to get any resolution. This whole situation had created a million and one questions for poor Saskia. All the police could do was fully investigate and pull on every thread.

When Saskia came back from the toilet, Zoe sat down with them.

'We need to talk about contact,' she said.

'No, no, no!' gasped Saskia in a panic. 'I don't want to see him! I can't be near him ever again! Please don't make me have contact with him!'

She was becoming hysterical. Zoe quickly stepped in.

'Saskia, it's OK,' Zoe soothed. 'I don't mean your dad, I promise. He's with the police right now. But now you're not seeing him, I wondered whether you wanted to use that contact session to see your mum?'

Rosa looked at her and squeezed her hand.

'Yes,' said Saskia with a weak smile. 'I'd like that.'

'Why can't she just come and see me at your house, Maggie?' she added. 'Why do we always have to go to that centre?'

'I would have loved that, sweetheart, but Maggie and Zoe have to follow the rules and I'd rather see you an extra day than not,' Rosa told her, squeezing her hand.

It was getting late now and I could see that Saskia was physically and emotionally exhausted. I was keen to get her back to the house.

'Saskia, lovey, I think it's probably time to go now,' I told her gently.

'No,' she said, suddenly throwing her arms around Rosa. 'No, I don't want to. I want to go back with you, Mum.'

'Sweetheart, I know it's hard but you have to go home with Maggie,' Rosa told her, gently stroking her hair.

'Maggie's house isn't my home,' she snapped. 'I want to be with you.'

'Saskie, that's very rude,' Rosa told her. 'You must apologise to Maggie. She's shown you nothing but kindness when I couldn't be with you.'

I stepped in.

'It's OK, Saskia is absolutely right,' I said. 'My house is not her home; she's just living with me at the moment while you can't look after her. I want her to feel comfortable in my house but I know that her true home is with you.'

'Thank you,' smiled Rosa.

She turned to Saskia. 'Sweetheart, you need to go back with Maggie now,' Rosa told her.

Saying goodbye was always hard for them but after what had happened today, I knew Saskia was going to struggle. It was heartbreaking for Rosa, too, and I was grateful to her for being so co-operative.

'I'll see you in a couple of days, at contact,' Rosa told her.

'That's right,' I nodded. 'It will fly by. Let's go back and have some dinner.'

I could see Saskia's bottom lip wobbling and she suddenly threw her arms around Rosa and started to sob.

'What if he did hurt me Mum? I can't stop thinking about it,' she wept.

'I know, sweetie,' she soothed. 'I can't either. But whatever happened in the past, you're safe now and it's going to be OK. Your dad can't hurt you any more.'

While they said their goodbyes, Zoe pulled me to one side. 'I'll keep in touch, Maggie, and let you know what's going on,' she told me in a low voice. 'The police said they'd keep me updated about James.'

'Thanks,' I replied.

Eventually, I managed to get Saskia out of the building.

'It's good that you had an extra visit with your mum, so you could talk directly to her rather than having to wait until later in the week,' I said.

Saskia nodded but she looked absolutely shattered.

I knew there was one subject I wanted to bring up on the drive home.

'Your mum said that you wanted a doctor to examine you,' I said. 'Are you comfortable with that happening soon?'

I wanted to check that Rosa hadn't put pressure on Saskia to do it and that she wanted to go through with it.

'I want to know what he did to me when I was asleep,' she nodded. 'Will my mum be able to come with me?'

'We want to make it as comfortable as possible for you and if it would help to have your mum there, then I'm sure Zoe would agree to it,' I reassured her.

For the rest of the drive, Saskia was very quiet while I talked about mundane things like what we were going to have for dinner and what we planned to do the following weekend. It had been an intense day and I thought Saskia could do with some light relief. I was exhausted and I knew she was too.

As soon as we walked through the door, I could feel my phone ringing in my bag. Saskia quickly disappeared off upstairs and I answered it, thinking it might be Zoe.

'Hi, Maggie,' said a voice.

It was Louisa. She just wanted to chat, but I didn't feel particularly talkative.

'I went up to Edie's nursery this afternoon for a concert,' she told me. 'They sang some songs – Edie was singing her little heart out – and then we were allowed to stay and play with them. It was so cute.'

'Aw, that sounds lovely,' I told her.

'You'll have to come to the next one,' Louisa told me. 'In fact, Edie asked if Nana was coming. I talked to the staff and they said grandparents are allowed to come along.'

'Oh, I'd love that,' I smiled.

'Are you OK?' Louisa asked. 'You sound a bit flat.'

'No, I'm fine, lovey, sorry,' I told her. 'It's just been a long day, that's all, and I've had a couple of difficult meetings.'

I knew at this stage that the situation with Saskia wasn't my information to share, and I found I was enjoying the sense of normality and hearing Louisa talk to me about everyday, ordinary things. After everything that had happened, I needed the distraction.

I was just getting our pizzas out of the oven when my phone beeped. I glanced down at my mobile on the work surface.

It was Zoe: *James been charged with possession of a Class A drug, possession of a Class B drug and making and possessing indecent images of a child. He's been bailed.*

I quickly typed out a reply.

Can I let Saskia know? I asked.

Yes, of course, she said.

I decided to leave it until the morning to tell her. I felt she was already struggling to process what had happened today without me adding to her worries. Sadly in my career I'd dealt with situations like this before where birth parents had been charged with neglecting or abusing their children. When it involved telling a younger child, it would usually be done through play therapy or life story work with their social worker. As Saskia was older, I felt it was better coming from me. It wasn't something that I ever enjoyed doing but I knew after everything that Saskia had been through, I needed to be brutally honest with her and she deserved to know the whole truth about her dad. Saskia was very quiet as we sat having dinner but I knew I needed to talk to her about school too.

'I know today has been really hard and upsetting,' I told her. 'But I think it would really help you if you could get back into some sort of normal routine so your mind's got something else to think about.'

Saskia shrugged.

'What do you think about going back to school tomorrow?' I asked her.

'Do I have to?' asked Saskia.

'No, but I really think it would help to distract you,' I told her. 'It would do you good to think about boring old maths – or what's that play you're doing in English?'

'*An Inspector Calls*,' she sighed.

'That's right,' I smiled. 'You need to think about *An Inspector Calls* and algebra.'

'OK,' said Saskia, giving me a weak smile. 'Maybe you're right.'

'Well, let's see how you feel in the morning,' I replied.

I was a firm believer that normality and routine helped children feel more secure when they were going through a difficult time.

That night, we watched a bit of TV together, although I don't think either of us were particularly concentrating on *The Parent Trap*.

'I think you ought to head to bed, lovey,' I told her just before nine. 'I'll come up with you.'

I went into her bedroom, closed her curtains and put her light on while Saskia brushed her teeth.

I popped my head around the bathroom door to find her standing in front of the mirror, sobbing.

'Oh, flower, are you OK?' I asked.

'I just don't understand,' she sobbed. 'Why did he do that to me? Why did he want to take those photos of me, Maggie?'

I took the toothbrush out of her hand, put it down on the side and gave her a hug.

'I don't understand it either,' I told her. 'What your dad did to you was very wrong and he needs to be punished.'

She nodded as I passed her a bit of toilet roll to blow her nose.

'I know it must be so hard for you to get your head around, and it's OK to cry and get upset and feel angry about it,' I told her.

'I am angry,' she said. 'I hate him for what he's done to me and Mum. Do you think he will be punished?'

'The police and the courts will have to decide that,' I nodded. 'But he's been charged with some really serious offences.'

Saskia nodded and I could see she was taking it all in. She looked exhausted.

'I think what you need now is a good night's sleep,' I added. 'Things will feel a little bit better in the morning.'

I took her to her bedroom, where she curled up under the duvet and I sat on the bed.

'You were really brave today, you know,' I told her. 'Braver than people much older than you. It must have been so hard for you having to listen to all of those upsetting things the police were telling you.'

She nodded and I could see her eyes filling with tears again.

'I don't think I can go to sleep,' she whimpered. 'I keep thinking about it over and over in my head, and I feel scared that something else is going to happen to me.'

'That is totally understandable, flower, but nothing is going to happen to you,' I told her. 'You're safe here – he can't hurt you any more.'

She nodded.

'Just close your eyes and try to get some sleep. I'll be right here if you need me, OK? I promise.'

I put my hand on hers.

'I'm so proud of you,' I told her. 'You've been so strong.'

It was often at bedtime that children felt upset when they were thinking about what had happened that day. For poor Saskia, today had been unbearably hard. She was absolutely drained but I really did hope she would be able to sleep.

I went downstairs and busied myself with tidying up. I went to check on her ten minutes later and poked my head around her bedroom door.

I gave a sigh of relief as I saw that she was fast asleep.

Today she had discovered horrific things about what her father had done to her. Hopefully the worst was over in uncovering any more shocking secrets, and now we had to deal with the aftermath and put Saskia – her health, happiness and future – first.

SIXTEEN

Searching for Answers

It wasn't just Saskia who was exhausted; I must have fallen asleep the minute my head had hit the pillow. In fact, it was a shock the next morning when my alarm went off at six thirty.

Thankfully Saskia had managed to get some sleep, but she still looked shattered. Her eyes were bloodshot and her face was puffy. I thought she might have changed her mind about going to school but I was relieved when she walked into the kitchen in her uniform. I hoped it would be good for her to be around her friends to try to take her mind off things.

Although I wasn't sure if that would change once I told her about the charges against James. It didn't feel right keeping information about her father from her, so I waited until she was sitting at the table to tell her what I had learnt.

'I had a text from Zoe,' I told her as we had breakfast. 'Your dad has been charged with possessing drugs and having indecent photos of you.'

'Good,' she nodded. 'So he's in prison now?'

'Not at the moment,' I replied. 'He's out on bail until he has to go to court.'

Saskia's face fell.

'What do you mean?' she gasped. 'Didn't they believe me?'

'It's not a question of believing you, lovey,' I told her. 'It's about the system and following a process. At some point, your dad will have to go to court and a judge or a jury will decide what will happen to him and what his punishment will be.'

'But if they believe me then why can't he go to prison now?' she asked.

These were difficult questions and I knew the legal system was confusing for children.

'The police and the courts have to follow a process,' I explained. 'And, at the minute, your dad is allowed to be out on bail.'

'But what if he comes for me?' she panicked. 'He'll be cross that I told the police about the drugs. What if he tries to hurt me?'

I explained that part of his bail conditions were that he had to stay away from both her and Rosa.

'He's not allowed to come anywhere near this house and Zoe has let school know what's happening,' I added. 'If he tries to come anywhere near you, we'll call the police and he'll immediately be arrested.'

Saskia looked genuinely terrified, but as she finished breakfast, I could see her resolve coming into force. Saskia continued to surprise me, and thankfully she still seemed keen to go to school. Nevertheless, as we got in the car, I could see she looked anxious.

'When we get there, do you want me to walk you in rather than dropping you off in the car park as normal?' I suggested.

'Yes, please,' she nodded.

As we drove up the long, winding drive that led to the main school building, I could see her looking around the grounds.

'Saskia, look at me, lovey,' I said. 'He's not going to be here.'

'How do you know?' she asked, her face crumpled with worry.

'The police have told him to stay away from you, and if he was here, your teachers would ring the police straight away,' I told her. 'And he would be arrested immediately because he would have broken the rules.'

However, I could see she was still nervous as we walked across the car park to the front entrance.

Zoe had already filled in the headteacher, Mrs Blackmore, about what had happened and she was there to meet us.

'I think Saskia's feeling a little bit anxious today,' I told her.

'Saskia, if you have any problems, come straight to me,' she told her.

'I'm sure it will be OK,' I smiled. 'Would you like me to come and pick you up from the office at home time, Saskia?'

'Yes, please,' she said.

She looked a little bit brighter as Mrs Blackmore walked her off to her tutor group.

Her school was being so supportive, but the reality was I didn't know how long she was going to be able to stay there. It was unlikely that James would continue to pay the fees if he went to prison. I knew it would be yet more upheaval for Saskia, but there wasn't a lot that we could do to get around it.

When I got home, I gave Vicky a ring. I felt like I needed to talk things through with someone not directly involved in the placement.

'Oh, Maggie,' she gasped when I told her everything that had unfolded over the past few days. 'Poor Saskia, that's horrific.'

'It really is,' I sighed.

'It's such a lot for her to cope with at thirteen,' she said.

'I know. I'm struggling to work out how to help her,' I said. 'I think all I can do is keep things as stable and as normal as possible, and at the same time try to answer any questions she might have as truthfully as I can.'

'What about counselling?' asked Vicky.

'She can talk to me or her social worker, but she can't access any proper therapy until all the legal proceedings are over,' I said.

I knew that if, further down the line, James pleaded not guilty, she would potentially have to go through a trial and possibly give evidence against her dad. If she started therapy then there was a risk that the more she talked about it, her recollections might start to change and differ from her original statement.

As the days passed, Saskia seemed to be coping quite well. I watched her like a hawk but she seemed happy to be going to school and her anxiety around James seemed to have eased a little.

Occasionally she'd need reassurance as things slowly started to sink in. Her questions would come out of nowhere when we were doing the most mundane of things. We were washing up one afternoon when she suddenly turned to me and asked: 'Is my dad going to go to prison?'

I knew I couldn't promise her anything so I had to be honest.

'What your dad did was very wrong but it's up to the courts to decide what his punishment will be,' I told her. 'And that might include prison.'

'What will happen to me?' she asked in a quiet voice. 'If Dad goes to prison and then Mum does too, where will I go?'

'That's up to you,' I said gently. 'I've told Zoe that I'm more than happy for you to stay here with me as long as you need to.'

'Can I?' she said. 'I don't need to go to a children's home like that boy?'

'PJ was in a children's home because me and a few other foster carers couldn't manage his behaviour,' I told her. 'I'm happy for you to stay here if you want to.'

'If my mum goes to prison, then I want to,' she nodded.

She looked relieved. I smiled and grabbed her hand and gave it a squeeze. I could see that she was constantly going over things in her mind and trying to work out what was going to happen. She had been through something huge and traumatic at such a young age, and I understood her need to have solid facts about her future to cling on to.

Before I knew it, it was Monday again and a week since we'd been at the police station. That morning, Zoe rang me.

'The police have authorised for Saskia to have an internal examination by a police doctor to see if there's any evidence that sexual abuse took place,' she told me.

'OK,' I said. 'Where do I have to take her?'

'I've spoken to DC Bangs and she suggested that it's done at the video interview suite at the police station where we went last week,' said Zoe.

'I suppose at least it will be somewhere familiar for Saskia,' I said.

Zoe said she was happy for me to take her and for Rosa to meet us there.

'I spoke to Rosa and she's keen to be there to support Saskia,' she added. 'It will be good for Rosa to be with her during the examination.'

'I agree,' I said.

It was a deeply distressing thing for any child to have to go through, but I knew having her mum there to hold her hand would comfort Saskia.

That night, when Saskia got home from school, I told her about it. Her face fell and she looked panicked.

'Where do I have to go?' she asked.

'We're going to go back to the same place at the police station we went to last week,' I told her. 'They've got an examination room there.'

'Will it hurt?' she asked.

'It might be a little bit uncomfortable, but it will all be over very quickly and the doctor will talk you through it,' I reassured her. 'Zoe said they'll make sure it will be a woman doctor.'

'But will everyone be able to see my bum?' she asked.

'No, the doctor will put a sheet over your bottom half so no one will be able to see anything,' I added. 'And your mum can come in with you.'

She still looked really worried.

'You don't have to do this, flower, but if you want to go ahead, you will get through it,' I told her. 'It'll be over before you know it.'

'I just want to know what he did to me,' she told me firmly.

'I know,' I replied. 'And I think you're being incredibly brave to make this choice.'

I could see how nervous she was about the examination but I admired her courage in putting herself through it.

'When do I have to go?' she asked.

'In a couple of days,' I told her. 'I'll let school know.'

'Will you have to tell them what it is?' she asked.

'Don't worry, I'll just say we have a doctor's appointment,' I told her.

All I could do to support her was to answer any questions she had over the next few days and just be there for her.

'At least I'll get to see my mum,' she sighed.

I was pleased that she was trying to focus on the positives.

On the day itself, I could see Saskia was torn apart by nerves. She'd had a disturbed night's sleep and just picked at a piece of toast.

'I don't want any breakfast,' she muttered, eventually pushing her plate away.

'It's going to be OK,' I told her. I had everything ready for her – coat, shoes – before we got into the car, but I didn't want her to feel pressured, so on the way there I kept talking about other things, like what we could bake together at the weekend, while reassuring her that her mum would be at the station.

When we got to the police headquarters, Rosa was already waiting for us in the reception area.

'Mum!' yelled Saskia, running towards her and giving her a hug.

'How are you doing, sweetheart?' Rosa asked her.

'I'm really scared, Mum,' Saskia told her, her bottom lip trembling.

'It's going to be OK,' replied Rosa. 'I'll be there to hold your hand.'

Eventually a blonde woman in jeans and trainers came out of the door and walked over to us.

'Hi,' she smiled, introducing herself. 'I'm Dr Frederica Alexander but you can call me Dr Freddie. And you must be Saskia. That's such a beautiful name.'

'Thanks. You don't look like a doctor,' Saskia told her.

'I'll take that as a compliment,' laughed Dr Freddie.

'This is Saskia's mum, Rosa,' I said. 'And I'm Maggie, Saskia's foster carer.'

'Great,' Dr Freddie smiled. 'Let's go through.'

Dr Freddie seemed very warm and smiley, and I could see that she'd instantly put Saskia at ease. They chatted as we walked down the corridors to the video interview suite.

'I've been here before,' Saskia told her. 'I came last week.'

'Oh, that's good,' smiled Dr Freddie. 'So you'll know exactly where you're going then.' She tapped us into the suite with her pass and we stood in the family room.

Saskia suddenly looked very nervous.

'Are you going to do it now?' she asked. 'Will it hurt?'

'Don't worry, it's going to be fine,' Dr Freddie told her. 'I'll talk you through everything and I promise it won't take long. I want you to be as comfortable as possible, and if you ever want me to stop, just let me know and I'll stop. Who's going to come in with you?'

'Rosa's going to stay with Saskia and I'll wait out here,' I told her.

'Great,' nodded Dr Freddie. 'Come through then, Saskia, and I'll show you my examination room. Maggie, there's tea and coffee on the side, so help yourself.'

'Thank you,' I nodded, although I didn't feel like drinking anything.

I didn't know what to do with myself while I waited. I started pacing up and down the family room, thinking about what was going on in the examination room.

When the door opened five minutes later, I was surprised that they'd finished so quickly. But it was Rosa on her own.

'Everything OK?' I asked. 'How's it going?'

Much to my surprise, she burst into tears.

'I said I needed the loo because I didn't want Saskia to see me crying,' she wept. 'I was trying to stay strong for her and hold it together but, honestly, I can't bear it, Maggie. How dare he do this to my little girl and have her go through this?' she sobbed. 'She's been through enough.'

'It's horrific,' I agreed. 'But it's important for Saskia to get some answers and for her to try to make sense of things.'

'It's the answers I'm scared of, Maggie,' Rosa sniffled. 'What if he *has* had sex with her? What do we do then? How do we even know it was just him?'

She was crying so much now she could hardly get her words out. I got her a tissue and put my arm around her shoulders.

'Rosa, let's deal with things when the time comes,' I told her. 'I know it's hard but let's just do what we can to get Saskia through today.'

'I'm really trying,' she sobbed. 'I just hate him for what he's done to us.'

I was conscious that Saskia was still in the examination room and needed someone by her side.

'Are you going to be OK or do you want me to go in and be with Saskia instead?' I asked.

'No, I'll go,' sniffed Rosa.

'Well, dry your eyes and try to get yourself together,' I told her gently but firmly. 'If Saskia sees you looking upset then she's going to get upset too.'

'I know,' Rosa said dejectedly.

Slowly, she started to calm down.

'That's better,' I smiled. 'Are you going to be OK?'

'I think so,' she nodded.

As she went back into the examination room, I really felt for her. She'd been through a lot too, but she needed to be strong for Saskia's sake.

It was another fifteen minutes before the door opened again and Rosa and Saskia walked out with Dr Freddie.

'All OK?' I asked and Saskia nodded.

'Saskia was so brave,' said Dr Freddie. 'I'll do a report and send it to your social worker. We should have the results in a couple of days.'

'How are you doing?' I asked her.

'It hurt a little bit but it wasn't too bad,' Saskia told me.

'The worst is over now,' I replied.

Over the next few days, I tried to keep everything as normal and stable as possible. Saskia kept asking me if I'd heard from Dr Freddie.

'Not yet, lovey,' I told her. 'Zoe will be in touch as soon as she hears anything.'

Three days later, Saskia had contact with Rosa at the centre. When I dropped her off, Zoe asked if I could stay as she wanted to have a quick word.

She sat in the contact room with Saskia, Rosa and I. 'I got the report from Dr Freddie today,' she told us.

Rosa looked like she was going to cry while Saskia stared down at the floor. My stomach started to churn.

'Please tell me he didn't touch her,' gasped Rosa.

'What did it say?' asked Saskia anxiously.

'There are no signs that penetration has taken place,' Zoe told us. 'The report said Saskia didn't have any internal bruising or scarring.'

'Thank goodness,' sighed Rosa.

'What does that mean?' asked Saskia.

'Dr Freddie doesn't think anyone had sex with you,' I told her. It was blunt but she needed to know what it meant in simple terms.

She looked relieved.

'That's good,' she nodded. 'So does that mean my dad didn't abuse me?'

'We can't rule out everything and sexual abuse can take many forms,' Zoe told her. 'He might have done other things like touching or some other inappropriate behaviour, but those kinds of things don't show up in any examination.'

It was a hard conversation to have but we had to be honest with her.

'But that's not fair!' yelled Saskia. 'I want to know what he did to me!'

'I know you do, lovey,' I told her, but I knew that unfortunately she may never truly know for sure. The only person who knew the truth was James and I feared he was never going to tell.

SEVENTEEN

A Waiting Game

Days passed and Saskia quietly got on with things. I thought the report from Dr Freddie would be preying on her mind and she'd still have lots of questions. However, whenever I tried to bring it up or mentioned anything about her dad, she quickly closed down the conversation.

I spoke to my supervising social worker Becky about it.

'Maybe she's had enough of talking about it?' she suggested. 'Perhaps she wants to try to forget about it for a while?'

'I think you're right,' I agreed.

Children often coped with a stressful situation by telling themselves it didn't exist, so they didn't have to think about it. Perhaps Saskia just needed a little space and time where nothing much happened?

School seemed to be going OK and she was still having contact with Rosa twice a week. So, instead of worrying that she was bottling things up, I tried to savour this small pocket of calm in case it didn't last for long.

★

One afternoon when I dropped Saskia at contact, Rosa was walking into the centre at the same time as us.

'Have you been shopping?' I asked, gesturing to the bags she was carrying.

'I'm at court tomorrow so I thought I'd better wear something smarter than jeans,' she replied.

Saskia pulled a face.

'Why didn't you tell me, Mum?' she gasped. 'Are you going to go to prison?'

'Don't worry, sweetheart,' Rosa explained. 'It's just a plea hearing where I tell a judge whether I'm pleading guilty or not guilty. Nothing much is going to happen.'

'But what are you going to say?' asked Saskia.

'I'm going to plead guilty,' Rosa told her. 'There's no point denying it – I *am* guilty. I took you to Spain without getting your dad's consent but I'm hoping that after everything that has come to light since, a judge will understand why.'

'I don't think they'll send you to prison, Mum,' Saskia told her. 'You were just protecting me. They'll know my dad is a horrible man.'

'I hope so, sweetheart,' she replied.

After Rosa and Saskia had gone into the contact room, I had a quick word with Zoe. I explained the conversation they'd just had.

'I'm worried Saskia doesn't think her mum's going to get a custodial sentence,' I told her. 'If Rosa does get sent down, it's going to be a huge shock for her.'

'Her lawyer has always said a custodial sentence is likely, so I think we have to prepare Saskia for that,' Zoe nodded.

'I'll talk to her later,' I said.

Later on the next day, Zoe forwarded me a text that she'd received from Rosa.

Court was OK, she'd written. *Judge has ordered pre-sentence reports so that's going to delay everything again. I just want to know what's going to happen to me.*

Things were creeping along at such a slow pace and I appreciated how hard and frustrating it was for her and Saskia not knowing what the future held.

'Your mum's got to wait a few more weeks before she can go back to court to be sentenced,' I told Saskia when I updated her after school.

'That's OK,' she nodded. 'She's not going to go to prison anyway.'

I took a deep breath.

'Saskia, we don't know that for sure,' I replied. 'Yes, your mum did what she did for a good reason but, even so, she did break the law.'

'But she can tell the judge what my dad did to me,' Saskia said. 'They will know he's not a very nice person.'

'That's true,' I said. 'But child abduction is a really serious charge and I don't want you to get your hopes up.'

Nobody knew what was going to happen but there was a real risk Rosa would still get a custodial sentence. Saskia had experienced so much, so naturally I didn't want to upset her any more, but it felt important to keep her in the loop. She was a smart thirteen-year-old, aware of what was going on, and with her mum, myself and Zoe around her, we all felt she had a support system that she could rely on.

★

While Rosa's court case was rumbling on, we were also waiting for news from the police about James.

Zoe tended to share any updates at contact sessions when everyone was together and Saskia had Rosa there to support her.

It was a few weeks later, in mid-December, before she had anything more to tell us.

'I had a call from DC Bangs today,' Zoe told us as we all sat in the contact room. 'She was ringing to let me know that James had a court hearing yesterday.'

She paused and I could tell from her sombre face that it wasn't going to be good news.

'Unfortunately, he's pleaded not guilty to all of the charges.'

'What?' gasped Rosa. 'How can he plead not guilty? How can he do this to us? He's put us through enough and even now he's managing to control and torment us.'

I was astounded too, and I felt that Rosa was probably right. It really did feel like James just wanted to cause more trauma for everyone.

'What does that mean?' asked Saskia, confused. 'How can he not be guilty when the police found drugs at our house and the photos? They showed them to me.'

I could see the utter despair in her face.

'Why won't they believe me?' she sighed. 'I've told everyone what it was like living in that house with him and they've got the proof.'

'I can understand how it must seem to you but it's not that people don't believe you,' nodded Zoe. 'Everyone believes you but sometimes people choose to plead not guilty, and they have the right to have a trial.'

'Sweetheart, you've been brave, so brave, and we all know that you're telling the truth,' sighed Rosa. 'Your dad is deluded. He doesn't want to face the consequences of his actions.'

My heart sank at the thought of there being a trial. It was a hard, stressful thing for any child to have to go through and it involved reliving everything again in front of a courtroom full of strangers.

Saskia had given a video statement when James was first arrested, but it was likely that she would have to give evidence and be cross-examined. Even if it was by video link, it would be difficult for her to be interrogated by a barrister who was there to pick holes in her evidence and discredit her. It would only add to Saskia's feelings that people didn't believe her.

'When will the trial be?' asked Rosa.

'We don't know at this stage,' replied Zoe. 'But DC Bangs said she'd set up a meeting for myself, Maggie and the CPS where we'd go through everything that will happen.'

'Try not to worry,' she added, turning to Saskia. 'We're all here for you.'

But I could tell from the look on her face that she didn't feel reassured.

A few weeks later, it was Christmas. I loved Christmas and Louisa had invited me and Saskia over to their flat to spend the day with her, Charlie and Edie. Nothing beat watching my little granddaughter open her presents and see her beam with joy as her chubby hands tore off the wrapping paper.

I could see Saskia didn't really feel like celebrating.

'Why can't I spend Christmas with my mum?' she asked.

I'd gone over it with her a few times and explained that, as Rosa was still involved in court proceedings, she still couldn't have unsupervised contact with Saskia, even on a day like today.

'That's why all of your contact sessions are held at the centre,' I told her.

'But why can't we bring her to Louisa's?' she asked.

'I can't just invite people to Louisa's flat, lovey, it's not my home,' I explained. 'And, as much as I really wish that I could, it would be against the rules for me to invite your mum to my house on Christmas Day as your contact sessions have still got to be supervised at a contact centre.'

Zoe had arranged it so that Saskia had a contact session with Rosa on Christmas Eve and she'd given her permission for a phone call on Christmas Day.

At the Christmas Eve contact session, Saskia had been very tearful.

'I just want to be with you,' she told Rosa.

'We can't be together this year, sweetheart, so we just have to make the best of it,' Rosa said. 'Hopefully next year will be different.'

'I hope so,' nodded Saskia.

'We'll be back together soon, sweetheart,' she reassured her. 'We'll make next Christmas really special.'

Louisa did her best to give us a lovely Christmas, even though I could tell Saskia's heart wasn't in it. Seeing Louisa with her own daughter on Christmas Day was always very poignant for me. I couldn't help but remember those first few Christmases that she'd spent with me after her parents died. She'd always get very upset remembering all those happy festive periods that she'd had with her parents, and Christmas was a very sad time of year for her for a long time. Now it was lovely seeing her making things special for Edie, and it was a joyful time once again now she had her own little family to celebrate with.

This year she did her best to make Saskia feel involved. I got her a hairdryer and some make-up, and Louisa got her some nice toiletries, and she played with Edie and her new doll's house while I helped Louisa and Charlie to make Christmas dinner.

In the afternoon, Saskia used my mobile to ring Rosa. I put it on speakerphone as I had to listen in on the call and I could tell Rosa was putting on a brave face.

'I'm having a quiet day,' she told Saskia. 'But I'm OK.'

'I miss you, Mum,' Saskia said.

I could see she was upset when she came off the phone.

'I can't believe my dad can do what he wants, but me and Mum can't even see each other,' she sighed. 'I hope he goes to prison for a very long time.'

I didn't say anything as it wasn't my place to comment, but I really hoped so too.

In the first week of the new year, we had the meeting about the trial at the police headquarters. DC Lizzie Bangs introduced Zoe and I to a woman called Sue from the CPS.

'I've been reading the background on the case and Saskia's been through a lot,' she said.

'She has,' I agreed. 'That's why the thought of her having to go through a trial is really worrying me.'

I knew that Zoe was also concerned about this.

'As she's a minor, we'll obviously put special measures in place,' Sue told us. 'She's old enough to be cross-examined and answer questions, but she'll be able to do that from the live link-up room at the court. So although she'll be able to see the judge, the defence and the prosecution barristers, she won't be able to see her dad.'

Sue also explained that Saskia would be assigned a police liaison officer who would be there to guide her through the whole process.

'I'm sure you've been through this with other children before, Maggie,' she said, 'but they'll talk Saskia through everything and answer any questions or worries that she might have. She can also have a tour of the court before the trial and see the link-up room for herself.'

'I know she's already very anxious about it,' I told her.

'We'll do everything we can to try to make it as comfortable as possible for her,' said Sue.

However, I was still worried about how this was going to affect Saskia. After school that night, I told Saskia what I'd discussed with Sue.

'You'll have a special person assigned to you who will talk you through everything and we can go and look at the court so you know where you'll be going on the day,' I told her.

'Will I have to see him, Maggie?' she asked me. 'I really don't want to have to sit in that wooden box and have him stare at me,' she said, as a few tears started to fall.

I could see she was genuinely frightened whenever James was mentioned.

'It won't be like it is on TV and in films,' I told her. 'You won't be going into the witness box. Because you're a child, you're allowed to give evidence from a separate room so your dad won't be able to see you.'

'But will I have to see him?' she asked.

'No,' I said. 'Don't worry, you won't be able to see him either.'

I knew it didn't matter how much reassurance I gave Saskia – her fear was palpable whenever we talked about the trial.

Over the next few weeks, as her visit to the court loomed, I could see Saskia becoming more and more anxious. I taught her some breathing exercises and I'd get her to do them with me to try to help her control her panic and remind her that she was safe.

One night, I was about to turn my light out when I heard a knock at my bedroom door.

'Maggie,' a voice whispered. 'My leg hurts.'

'Let's go back to your room and have a look at it,' I told Saskia as I opened the door.

I went through the motions and asked her to sit on her bed and show me where it hurt, but I knew it wasn't really about her leg.

'Were you struggling to get to sleep?' I asked her and she nodded. She'd been in bed for over an hour by now.

'At the trial, will you be allowed to be with me?' she asked suddenly. It was clear she'd been worrying about going to court.

'I'll take you to court,' I explained. 'And even though I'm not allowed to be with you when you give your evidence, I'll be waiting right outside.'

'Will I be on my own?' she asked.

I shook my head.

'You'll have your liaison officer with you, who we'll meet next week,' I told her. 'And you can take a break whenever you need to. Everyone's going to be doing their best to make you feel as comfortable as possible.'

She nodded, but again I couldn't help thinking that no matter how many times we tried to reassure her, it didn't seem to be easing her worries.

A few days later, Saskia's headteacher, Mrs Blackmore, called me.

'I wanted to have a quick chat with you about Saskia,' she told me. 'A few of her teachers have commented that she's been a bit tearful recently.'

She also explained that she'd been very jumpy.

'She just seems on edge all the time,' she sighed. 'I said hello to her the other morning and she nearly jumped out of her skin. She was like a rabbit caught in headlights.'

I explained that the impending trial and visit to the court was causing her a lot of stress.

'As I'm sure you know, when children are stressed, they're on hyper alert,' I told her. I explained that I was trying to keep things as calm and consistent at my house as I could.

'And we're doing the same here at school,' Mrs Blackmore told me.

It would clearly be a team effort to support Saskia through the next few difficult weeks.

On the day that Saskia was due to go to the court to look around, I could see that she was very nervous. As we drove to school, her eyes were wide and flitting from her lap to the window to her lap again. She couldn't seem to focus on anything and I was becoming increasingly worried about the impending trial.

When I pulled up into the car park and turned off the engine, she burst into tears.

'What is it, flower?' I asked, although in my heart I already knew.

'I'm so scared,' she sobbed. 'What if I can't do it? Does that mean he'll get off?'

'You *will* be able to do it,' I assured her. 'You are strong. All you need to do is tell the truth.'

I could only hope that things wouldn't seem as scary for her once she'd seen the court.

'I'll see you after school for the court visit,' I told her. 'It's going to be OK, Saskia. You'll have me and your mum around you – we'll be with you every step of the way.'

But she looked terrified as I walked her into the school building.

I knew I needed to distract myself for the rest of the day so I didn't keep worrying about Saskia. It was Louisa's day off, so I spent the morning at a soft play centre with her and Edie. Edie was old enough to do a lot if it herself so it gave me and Louisa a chance to chat.

'I'll get us a coffee,' I said.

'I think I'll just have a mint tea,' she told me. 'I'm trying to cut down on coffee at the minute.'

Once we'd got our drinks, we sat and chatted. I knew I could talk to her in confidence so I told her about James's court case.

'Poor Saskia,' she sighed. 'I can't believe her own father is making her go through this.'

'I know. We're going to look at the court later so I'm hoping that will help to reassure her, otherwise she's going to spend the next few weeks worrying about the trial.'

'I hope it goes OK, Maggie,' said Louisa, giving me a hug as I left half an hour later. 'I'll be thinking of you both.'

'Thanks, lovey,' I replied, giving her a weak smile.

I drove home, made a sandwich and did some tidying up, then got in the car to go and collect Saskia from school so we could head to the court.

I'd just put my seatbelt on when I heard my phone ringing in my handbag. I quickly grabbed it. It was Zoe.

'Hi,' I said. 'I'm just leaving now to go and collect Saskia.'

'Maggie, there's been a change of plan,' she told me. 'I've just heard from the police. James has changed his plea. He's decided to plead guilty.'

It took a couple of seconds for what she was saying to fully sink in.

'What?' I gasped. 'How come?'

'I don't know, I just had a call from DC Bangs. She'd heard from his lawyer.'

It was a huge relief, but I was also furious.

'What cruel mind games is he playing?' I said, infuriated. 'Does he know how distressed Saskia has been these past few weeks, worrying about going to court? She's all psyched up for the visit today.'

At least he had seen sense but, as I drove to collect Saskia, I felt more and more angry with him as I thought of what he had put his daughter through. However, I knew my job was to deliver the news to her in a calm, factual way.

Saskia was sat in reception waiting for me. She looked exhausted from a lack of sleep and I could see the worry in her eyes.

'How long will it take us to get to the court?' she asked. 'Will we be there for a long time?'

I didn't want to tell her such significant news in the school reception area with lots of other people around us.

'Let's get in the car and we can have a look,' I said, ushering her out.

In the car, I waited for her to get in and shut her door before I turned to her.

'Saskia, there's been a bit of a change of plan,' I told her.

'What do you mean?' she asked suspiciously.

'Zoe called me earlier,' I explained. 'Your dad's changed his plea to guilty so you won't have to go to court any more.'

'Really?' she gasped. 'But why?'

'I don't really know,' I admitted. 'Zoe just had a call from the police.'

'But what if he changes it back again?' she asked.

'I don't think he can just keep doing that,' I told her.

'Are we still going to the court?' she asked.

'There's no point,' I shrugged. 'You won't have to give evidence now.'

I could see Saskia was churning everything over in her mind.

'I hate him,' she wept. 'I hate him so much. I've been so scared and worried about it. Why didn't he say this earlier?'

I could see that she was so angry at her dad and, to be honest, I was too.

EIGHTEEN

Justice

Rosa was equally as angry as Saskia at James's U-turn.

'How could he do that to us?' she sighed when Zoe told her the news at contact. 'How dare he put Saskia through the stress of all that?'

'But it means I don't have to go to court now, Mum,' Saskia told her.

'Well, I suppose at least he did the right thing in the end,' Rosa admitted.

Zoe explained that now James had pleaded guilty, he would go back to court in a few weeks to be sentenced. Coincidentally, it was the same situation Rosa was also facing.

'I want to be there,' Rosa said adamantly. 'I want to be there in court to look him in the eyes when he gets sent to prison.'

'That's completely up to you,' Zoe told her. 'Anyone can go into the public gallery of a court.'

I glanced at Saskia, half expecting her to ask if she could go too, but she didn't say anything. I was relieved as I wasn't sure it was a good idea. At the end of the day, she was still only thirteen and this was her dad, and there might be details about the images of her that she would find difficult and upsetting to hear.

Saskia didn't say anything else about it at contact. But on the drive home, she turned to me.

'I don't want to go to court to see my dad,' she said. 'But will you go instead? Then you can look after my mum and tell me what happens.'

It wasn't normally something a foster carer got involved in, but if it would help Saskia then I was willing to do it. Saskia was such a kind, caring girl, always looking out for her mum.

'I'll have to run it past Zoe,' I told her.

When Saskia was at school the following day, I gave Zoe a quick call and told her what she'd asked me to do.

'Is it OK with you if I go to James's sentencing?' I asked her.

'If you're comfortable with it, then that's fine by me,' she told me. 'I'll talk to Rosa and make sure she's happy with that too.'

She messaged me back later to say Rosa was relieved that I was going.

I think she appreciates the support, she wrote.

The sentencing had been scheduled for a few weeks' time. Although Saskia no longer had the trial to worry about, I could see she was equally as nervous about the sentencing.

On the morning of the court case, Saskia was clearly on edge.

'Will you be able to pick me up from school and tell me what's happened?' she asked anxiously.

'Yes,' I nodded. 'I'm going straight to the court after I've dropped you off at school and it should all be over by lunchtime. Sentencing hearings don't usually take that long.'

'OK,' she nodded.

I could see she was going over everything in her head.

'But what if they let him off, Maggie?' she asked me.

From what the police had said, I didn't think it was likely, but I couldn't promise Saskia that James was definitely going to go to prison.

'Let's cross that bridge when we come to it,' I told her. 'Let's not worry about something that might not happen.' I squeezed her hand. 'But whatever does happen, it will be OK. Your dad has admitted his guilt so we know he'll be given some sort of punishment.'

I hoped with all my might that James would go to prison for what he'd done, but a judge might feel he should make amends in a different way. I didn't want Saskia to be bitterly disappointed and I knew that I had to manage her expectations.

I'd arranged to meet Rosa outside the crown court. It was a big red-brick building built in the 1980s that I'd been to a few times before, over the years.

As I walked up the steps to the front entrance, I could see Rosa waiting for me outside. She looked exhausted.

'I'm dreading this – I couldn't sleep last night, worrying about seeing him. I don't know how I'll cope if he doesn't get a prison sentence,' she said, twiddling the rings on her hands. 'How can I go to prison and he doesn't? He's probably thrown money at the best barrister he can find who will be able to get him leniency.'

She was frantic and jittery, and with her questions coming thick and fast, she reminded me of Saskia. I felt sorry for Rosa; her own sentencing was just weeks away and she had a lot to cope with.

'It's in the judge's hands now,' I told her. 'There's nothing we can do.'

Rosa slumped back against the building wall.

'Are you OK?' I asked her.

'It just feels like there's a heavy weight on my chest, Maggie, and my heart is absolutely racing,' she told me. 'I think I might be sick. What if I'm sick in court?'

She did look very pale and clammy.

I led her away from the entrance and over to a nearby bench.

'Take a few deep breaths,' I told her, handing her a bottle of water from my bag.

She nodded as she took the bottle with a trembling hand.

'I know it's hard but try to stay calm,' I told her. 'We're doing this for Saskia.'

'I just want justice for her,' Rosa said. 'Those disgusting photos were bad enough, but who knows what else he did to her?'

She started to cry and collapsed in my arms. As a foster carer, children in the care system were my priority, but sometimes you found yourself in situations like this where birth parents also needed your care and support.

'It's going to be OK,' I soothed. 'Whatever the outcome is today, you and Saskia will cope. You have each other.'

'I hope so,' she wept.

Slowly, Rosa's breathing began to regulate and she started to calm down.

'Thank you, Maggie,' she told me. 'I've been going over and over everything in my mind and I think I worked myself up into such a frenzy.'

I looked at my watch.

'I don't want to rush you, but I think we'd better head in,' I told her.

'OK,' she nodded, taking another swig of water.

We walked into the reception area of the court and put our bags through a security scanner. There was an information desk where we could find out which court the sentencing hearing was taking place in.

'It's court six,' I told Rosa as I looked down the listings.

We walked along the corridor and I pushed open the heavy door to court six. It was a small court and there were only a couple of people in there. I recognised one of them as James's lawyer, Harry Chambers. He was talking to another man in a black gown, who I assumed must be James's barrister.

Rosa looked ashen when she saw him.

'Let's go and sit down in the public gallery,' I said, steering her towards the two rows of seats at the back of the courtroom.

'I don't think I can do this,' she whispered.

'You don't have to put yourself through this, you know,' I told her. 'I can stay for the sentencing and tell you what happens if you'd rather wait outside?'

Rosa shook her head. 'Thanks, Maggie, but for my own sake, I think I need to be here. I need to see it with my own eyes.'

I could feel Rosa tensing up next to me as a door opened and James walked into the court. He looked as well groomed as ever in a smart grey suit with his hair slicked back. He made my skin crawl.

When he looked up and saw Rosa, he smiled.

'I hate him,' she muttered. 'Grinning like a Cheshire Cat because he doesn't think he's going to prison.'

I tried not to look at him because when I thought about what he'd done to Saskia, it made my blood boil.

'All rise,' said the court clerk a few minutes later and we all stood as the judge entered the court in his wig and gown. He was in his fifties with a grey beard and glasses, and I hoped the stern look on his face meant that he'd come down hard on James.

As the prosecution barrister outlined the facts of the case, I deliberately tried to think about something else. I could handle the information about the drugs, but I thought it would be too upsetting to hear the details about the indecent images of Saskia. There were some things I just didn't want to know. I could see Rosa was the same.

As the prosecutor spoke, she sobbed quietly next to me.

'My poor baby,' she wept. 'How could he do that to her?'

I grabbed her hand and gave it a squeeze.

Then it was James's barrister's turn to speak.

'Your Honour, Mr Bradbury knows what a devastating impact his crimes have had. Primarily, and most devastatingly to him, on his beloved daughter with whom his relationship has been destroyed forever by his despicable actions. For my client, that is the greatest punishment of all.'

Rosa shook her head.

'There are no words that can adequately convey his shame and remorse for what has happened,' the barrister continued. 'My client was heavily under the influence of drugs when the images were taken and he can't recollect anything about them.

'All he can do is apologise and admit his guilt. He's a first-time offender and has never been the subject of any court proceedings before. He's currently enrolled in a rehab programme to get clean and sober, and wants to assure you that he will never take illegal substances again.'

While his barrister was speaking, James stood upright in the dock, nodding his head.

'Don't let him trick his way out of prison,' muttered Rosa. 'He's not the good man that he likes people to think he is.'

The judge flicked through the pile of papers that he had in front of him before he began to speak.

'Your attempts at rehabilitation and therapy are admirable, as is your guilty plea,' he stated. 'However, I have to take into consideration the seriousness of your crimes. In particular, the creation and possession of the indecent images of your own daughter, which has understandably had a devastating impact on her life and is a crime most despicable in nature. Your job as a father is to love and protect her, not to exploit her in the most deviant of ways.'

Rosa grabbed my hand with a vice-like grip. My heart was beating out of my chest and I could hardly focus on what the judge was saying because the same five words were running through my head.

Please send him to prison. Please send him to prison. For Saskia's sake, please send him to prison.

The judge's voice filtered back into my consciousness.

'. . . I therefore sentence you to five years in prison.'

Suddenly I was aware that Rosa had stood up next to me.

'I hope you rot in there,' she shouted at James. 'How could you do that to my baby girl, you disgusting monster.'

James glared up at her and then he burst out laughing.

'Aren't you going to prison soon?' he scoffed. 'I'll probably be out before you, you mad cow. And then Saskia can come and live with me.'

'Don't you dare say that!' shouted Rosa. 'I'll never let you near her again!'

'We'll see,' shrugged James.

A few seconds later, he was led away by two security guards.

Rosa collapsed back down into her seat and burst into tears.

'I hate him,' she sobbed. 'I really hate him.'

'Rosa, he's just goading you,' I told her. 'Social Services would never allow Saskia to go to live with him again. He's a horrible man.'

I put my hand on her arm.

'You've got what you wanted,' I told her. 'I can go home and tell Saskia that he's going to prison.'

'I know,' she wept. 'I know.'

We walked out of court together.

'Give Saskia my love and a big hug from me,' Rosa said. 'I'm sad that I can't tell her myself.'

'I will,' I told her. 'And she'll see you in a couple of days at contact.'

Later that afternoon I went to pick Saskia up from school. I usually walked to reception to collect her but she was already waiting on the front steps for me. She jumped up when she saw my car pull in. Then she came over and got in.

'Well?' she asked. 'What happened?'

'It's good news,' I told her. 'The judge sent your dad to prison for five years.'

'Good,' she nodded. 'I'm glad. He shouldn't have done that to me.'

I could see her going over it in her head.

'Did he say why he drugged me?' she asked.

'They didn't mention that, flower,' I told her. 'We all know that that's probably what happened but the police couldn't prove it, so he was never charged with that.'

It was so hard for her to understand and it must have seemed very unfair.

'I'll never know what he really did to me, will I?' she asked.

I shook my head.

'But you know that your dad's in prison and he can't hurt you any more,' I told her. 'You and your mum are safe and you've got each other.'

Saskia's eyes suddenly filled with tears.

'But we haven't though, have we?' she sighed. 'Mum's going to go to prison and then I'll have no one.'

'You've got me,' I smiled, putting my arm around her. 'Whatever happens, we'll get through this,' I told her. 'I promise you.'

NINETEEN

Courage and Cowards

In a cruel twist of fate, a few weeks after James's sentencing, Rosa found herself summoned back to the same court for her own hearing.

'At least we'll know what's going to happen to me,' she told Saskia after she'd broken the news to her at contact.

Saskia clung to her and became very tearful.

'I really don't want you to go to prison,' she wept. 'It's not fair.'

'Whatever happens, we'll deal with it and we'll get through it together,' Rosa told her.

The past few weeks had been an emotional rollercoaster for Saskia; now that the court proceedings were over for James, she had been able to start some counselling. She had an hour once a week at a local CAMHS (Child and Adolescent Mental Health Services) centre. Depending on the children's ages and needs, they had all sorts of counsellors there, from play therapists to psychologists. Saskia had been seeing a woman in her early thirties called Pippa, who she'd instantly bonded with.

I'd sat in on the first session where they'd introduced themselves and Pippa had talked to Saskia about what she wanted to get out of the sessions. From then on, she'd been comfortable enough to have them on her own.

It was really important for Saskia to have a private, safe space away from my house to talk about whatever she wanted. Sometimes children don't want to talk to a foster carer because they're with you all the time.

Saskia's sessions with Pippa seemed to be helping. Although she would be very quiet straight after them, over the following days she would gradually share with me some of what they'd talked about. I was pleased that she had someone to help her get through the next few weeks leading up to Rosa's sentencing as I knew it was going to be hard for her.

She came out of a session one afternoon clutching a sheet of paper.

'How's it gone today?' I asked her.

'Good,' she nodded. 'Pippa helped me to write these.' She held up a sheet of A4 paper.

'What have you got there?' I asked.

'It's a list of questions that I want to ask my dad.'

'Oh,' I said, surprised.

'You can read them if you want,' Saskia told me. 'I don't mind.'

I looked at the sheet where there was a short list of questions.

Why did you take photos of me?
Did you show anyone else the photos?
Did you give me drugs?
Why did you give me drugs?

Did you do anything to me when I was asleep?
Why did you do these things to me?

'They're all really good questions,' I said. 'Did it make you feel better to write them all down?'

In my experience, it helped children to write things down. It was a good way of easing their anger or sadness about something. I'd often get children to write down their feelings, then we'd burn the paper or rip it up. It was a good technique to help them process their upset.

'It helped me to write them all down,' nodded Saskia. 'Then when I see my dad, I can ask him those questions.'

At first, I thought I'd misheard her.

'Remember, Saskia, your dad is in prison and you don't have to see him ever again if you don't want to,' I told her.

'I've talked to Pippa about it and I've decided I want to see him,' she revealed. 'I want to ask him all these things, otherwise I'll never know.'

I was flabbergasted.

'Are you sure?' I asked. 'You'd have to go into the prison and see him.'

'Yep,' Saskia replied. 'Pippa said it might mean I'm not frightened of him any more.'

I didn't know how to respond to Saskia, but I wasn't sure that it was a good idea. My worry was that it was too soon, or it would upset her even more if James told her something that she didn't want to hear.

'OK. It's something that you need to talk to Zoe about,' I told her. 'And she'll have to check that your mum is happy too.'

She nodded. 'I will.'

Saskia seemed very determined about it. So determined, in fact that she mentioned it as soon as she saw Zoe at the next contact.

Rosa's face dropped when she heard Saskia's request.

'You want to do what?' she gasped. 'Why would you want to see that monster again?'

'I want to ask him why he did those things to me,' Saskia told her. 'I don't like not knowing.'

Rosa looked upset. 'Surely she can't be allowed to do that?' she asked Zoe.

'If Saskia wants to do it then I can look into it for her,' Zoe replied. 'James would have to agree to see her, and I could then apply to the courts for a visiting order.'

'He's a coward,' said Rosa. 'James will never agree to it.'

'I want to try, Mum,' Saskia told her.

I was worried too. For all of her bravado, I was concerned about how Saskia would react to seeing James again. But she was thirteen so we had to listen to her wishes, and we could all see how important it was to her. Perhaps it would help with her anxiety if she knew the truth?

Zoe called me a few days later and said that she'd spoken to Pippa about it.

'She feels that Saskia's strong enough to manage it,' she told me. 'So I've contacted the prison and put the request in.'

I hoped that perhaps Saskia would forget about it or change her mind. However, every few days, she asked if Zoe had any news.

Ten days later, Zoe called me.

'James has agreed to see Saskia,' she told me. 'I'm genuinely shocked.'

When I told Saskia the news, I think she was too.

'You don't have to go through with this, you know,' I reminded her. 'We'd all understand if you've changed your mind, or you wanted to do it at a later point.'

'No, I haven't,' she said firmly. 'I want to see him.'

I explained that Zoe would apply to the prison for two visiting orders. One for me and one for Saskia. Zoe wouldn't need one as she was classed as a professional and it was deemed as a work visit.

Rosa still wasn't on board with the idea.

'I just don't think it will do her any good,' she sighed. 'I think it will traumatise her to see that monster.'

'It's Saskia's decision,' Zoe told her. 'Maggie and I will be with her at all times and if she gets distressed, we'll cut the visit short.'

The visiting orders came through in a few days and I organised for Saskia to have the day off school, as the prison was a couple of hours away.

'I'll drive us there, and Zoe and I will both come into the visitors' room with you to see your dad,' I told her.

Despite all her confidence, as the visit approached, I could see Saskia was getting more and more jittery about it.

I talked her through what was probably going to happen and encouraged her to ask questions.

'Have you been to a prison before, Maggie?' she asked me.

'Yes, sadly quite a few times,' I nodded. 'The staff are very nice to children visiting, and they try to make things as comfortable as possible for you because they realise that it can feel scary.'

'Dad won't be able to hurt me, will he?' she asked. 'He'll be behind a big screen, won't he, and he can talk to me on a phone?'

'Saskia, I think you've been watching too many American films,' I smiled. 'It won't be like that where your dad is.'

I described how we'd see James in a visitors' room.

'Normally, this is a big room with lots of tables and chairs,' I explained. 'There tends to be prison officers dotted around and they keep an eye on things and make sure everyone is safe and happy.'

Because Saskia was a minor, I explained that this would be a special visit arranged outside of the normal visiting hours. I described how visiting times tended to be very overwhelming. You had to queue up to get in and the visitors' room sometimes got very hot and noisy.

'This will just be you, me, Zoe and your dad and probably a couple of prison officers.'

Saskia nodded but she looked terrified.

On the morning of the prison visit, she was up and dressed by 7 a.m.

'You're early,' I smiled. 'We don't need to leave for an hour or so.'

'I wanted to be ready,' she replied. 'I've got my questions.'

I could see how important it was for her to do go through with this and I admired her strength and determination.

Saskia was very quiet on the drive there and I didn't push her to chat. This was an incredibly brave thing for her to do and I was hoping that whatever answers James gave her, it would help her process things in some way.

As we pulled up outside the prison, I could see her staring out of the window.

'Here we are,' I said.

I drove into the car park where I could see Zoe in her car waiting for us. We pulled up next to her.

'Hi, Saskia,' she smiled as we all got out. 'All set?'

Saskia nodded and I could see she was understandably very nervous. To be honest, most people felt nervous going into a prison. No matter how many times I'd been in one, I know I always did. There was something about the atmosphere in them and the lack of daylight that made it feel very oppressive and I'd feel stressed and claustrophobic.

This prison was a very old one dating back to the late 1800s. There was a huge door at the front of it but we went through the visitors' entrance at the side.

As I'd hoped, there weren't lots of people waiting as it was outside of the usual visiting times.

Zoe buzzed us in.

'Will my dad answer the door?' Saskia asked.

'No, lovey,' I said. 'We have to go through security first.'

I explained how we'd have to show photo ID and our bags would be searched.

'One of the guards will probably want to pat us down to make sure we're not smuggling anything into the prison,' I told her.

'Like what?' Saskia asked.

'Something illegal like drugs or a weapon,' Zoe explained.

Saskia's eyes widened.

Thankfully it was a female security guard who searched us and she was very gentle and considerate with Saskia, which I appreciated. We had to take our shoes off and she pulled our bras out to check that we weren't hiding anything in them.

'Can you take your bobble out, darling,' she asked Saskia, gesturing to her ponytail.

Saskia looked confused.

'You need to take your hair down,' I explained.

'But why?' she asked.

'Some people hide drugs or other banned things in their hair and they need to check it,' Zoe told her.

I'd been to prisons with babies and toddlers before, and the guards had made me change their nappies in front of them before we went in to check I wasn't hiding anything.

After we'd had all of the security checks, we were shown to a waiting area.

'We'll take you through to the visitors' room shortly, then we'll bring Mr Bradbury from his cell,' one of the prison officers told us.

Saskia was clearly still very nervous, fidgeting and rereading her list of questions.

'It's going to be OK,' I told her, putting my hand on her arm.

When the prison officer came back through to us, she jumped up.

'I'll take you through now,' he said.

The heavy security door buzzed open and we followed him down a long, bare corridor that smelt of bleach. There were only tiny slits along the top of the walls for windows so there was harsh strip lighting.

'OK?' I asked Saskia.

She suddenly grabbed my hand and I gave it a squeeze.

The officer led us into a large visitors' room that was currently empty.

'Sit wherever you want,' he smiled.

We picked one of the tables that had a chair one side and four chairs at the other side of the table. They were all attached to the floor, which I knew was so no one could throw them.

'My colleague will go and get Mr Bradbury now,' the officer told us.

Saskia looked around the room nervously.

'How long have I got with my dad?' she asked Zoe.

'Up to an hour,' answered Zoe. 'But we don't have to stay that long and we can leave at any time.'

We came up with a phrase that Saskia could say if she wanted to leave but didn't feel brave enough to say 'I want to go' in front of her dad.

'Why don't you say, "Maggie, please can we go and get some crisps?"' I suggested. 'Then Zoe and I will know that you want to leave, and we can tell your dad that we have to go.'

'That sounds like a good plan,' Zoe told her.

I could see Saskia staring anxiously at the door that the prison officer had gone out of.

'How long do you think he'll be?' she asked, looking at her list of questions again.

'I don't honestly know,' I shrugged. 'Prisons are big places so it might take a while to get your dad from his cell and bring him back here.'

So we waited. And we waited. I looked at my watch.

Over half an hour had passed and there was still no sign of the prison officer or James.

'I'll go and see what's happening,' Zoe said.

She went over to the officer seated on the other side of the room doing some paperwork.

'He doesn't know,' she said when she came back. 'He said they're probably on their way.'

Saskia didn't say anything but the poor little mite looked scared to death.

Suddenly there was a clatter and all of our gazes shot to the security door. As it buzzed open, my heart started racing in anticipation of seeing James and I felt Saskia reaching for my hand again.

However, I was confused when the prison officer walked back into the visitors' room alone.

'Where is he?' whispered Saskia. 'Where's my dad?'

He walked over to the other officer and said something in a low voice. Then he came over to us. I knew instantly there was something wrong.

'I'm afraid Mr Bradbury isn't coming today,' he told us. 'He's refusing to leave his cell.'

'What?' gasped Saskia. 'But why?'

'He said he doesn't feel up to seeing any visitors today.'

'But that's not fair,' she sighed. 'We've come all this way.'

I could see how upset and bitterly disappointed she was. It had taken so much courage to come here today to confront her dad and she'd got herself all psyched up.

'Why would he agree to a visit and get me to come all the way over here if he wasn't going to see me?' asked Saskia.

'Mind games,' sighed Zoe. 'He's showing you that he still has the power and the upper hand.'

Saskia burst into tears.

'I hate him,' she sobbed. 'I don't ever want to see him again.'

She got her list of questions and scrunched it up into a ball. She was utterly dejected and I was relieved that she had a counselling session with Pippa the following day. Hopefully she would talk Saskia through it and help her to process it all.

'Come on,' I sighed. 'Let's go home.'

As the prison officer walked us back to the entrance, we passed a bin. Saskia threw her list of questions into it.

'I'm never going to know what he did to me, am I, Maggie?' she asked.

'I know it's hard but rather than focus on the past, you have to look forward now,' I told her.

TWENTY

Flying Free

Rosa stood in the dock, tears streaming down her face. As the prosecution barrister went through the charges against her, she dabbed her eyes with a tissue.

It was a different courtroom this time to the one we'd been in to see James being sentenced. As Zoe and I sat in the public gallery, what struck me was the difference between them both. I remembered James's arrogant swagger in the dock compared to Rosa, who I could see was physically shaking with fear.

It was a female judge deciding Rosa's fate, and I hoped that meant she would have compassion for her because of what she'd been through.

'Mrs Bradbury would like to say a few words to you, Your Honour, before you pass sentencing,' Rosa's barrister told the judge.

'Well, it's not something a defendant would usually do, but on this occasion I'll allow it,' the judge said with a stern look on her face.

Rosa cleared her throat, and I could tell how nervous she was.

'I just wanted to say how sorry I am,' she sniffed, her voice quivering. 'I know it was wrong to take my daughter out of the country, but I didn't know what else to do. I was desperate – all my instincts were telling me I needed to get her away from my ex-partner and I was right.

'For the past four months, Saskia has been in care and I'm begging you, please give us a chance to be together. I want to be with my baby girl again. She's been through enough. She needs her mum. We need to heal together.'

The judge looked over her glasses at Rosa.

'I think I've heard enough,' she nodded.

Her tone was firm and I was worried that Rosa's pleas had had the opposite effect. I knew it would break Saskia's heart if her mum had to go to prison for the next few years, but it was a reality we were now facing.

The judge shuffled through the papers in front of her. My stomach was churning with nerves. Poor Rosa looked like she was about to collapse as she held on to the sides of the dock for support as the judge began to speak.

Zoe shot me a nervous glance.

'When you took your daughter to Spain, you clearly knew that you were breaking the law,' the judge told her.

Rosa nodded. Her face was now swollen and red from crying.

The judge paused.

'However, you clearly know your own child and you could see something wasn't right when she came back from spending time with her father. And sadly those instincts were right and, as we have heard today, your ex-partner is now serving a prison sentence.'

She looked up at Rosa.

'I think your daughter has been through enough. I feel it would be more a punishment for her if I were to impose a custodial sentence on you today. And so, for that reason, I sentence you to six months in prison suspended for twelve months. I wish you and your daughter all the best.'

Zoe and I beamed at each other in relief while Rosa stood in the dock, looking stunned. Everyone stood as the judge left the courtroom.

'What just happened?' she gasped. 'Am I going to prison?'

'No, you're most certainly not,' her barrister told her.

'What, I'm free to go?' she said incredulously.

'I think it's going to take a while for it to sink in,' I told Zoe, still smiling.

Rather than being ecstatic, Rosa just looked shocked and exhausted.

We walked over to the dock to chat to her while the barristers packed up their things.

'I think I need to sit down for a minute,' she sighed. 'I can't take it all in.'

'You're free to go,' Zoe told her. 'Let's get you out of here and go and get you a cup of tea.'

Rosa looked like her legs were going to give way as she followed us to the café in the court building.

'I can't honestly believe it!' she said, sitting down. 'I was expecting the worst. I even had my bag packed for prison,' she said, gesturing to the black holdall by her feet.

'It'll probably take a while to sink in,' Zoe told her.

'I need to tell Saskia,' Rosa said. 'I can't wait to see her face.'

Saskia had been keen to come to court for the sentencing, but Rosa had asked her not to. She didn't want to put her through more trauma and upset by potentially seeing her mum being sent to prison.

'Please just go to school as normal,' she'd told Saskia. 'Don't worry – Zoe and Maggie will update you about what happens as soon as possible.'

Reluctantly, Saskia had agreed.

Zoe had organised for a taxi to pick Saskia up from school and take her to the contact centre where we had arranged to meet her after the sentencing. Even if Rosa wasn't there and had gone to prison, we could use the session to break the news to Saskia and talk to her about how she felt.

The sentencing had happened in the afternoon, so we went straight to the contact centre to wait for Saskia.

'She's going to be so happy to see you,' I told Rosa. 'Over the last few days, I think she'd been preparing herself for the worst.'

She'd been very tearful and struggling to sleep.

I sat in the contact room with Rosa while Zoe waited in reception for Saskia.

'I can see her taxi pulling up,' she called.

I got up and looked out of the window, which had the type of glass that meant you couldn't see in from the outside, but you could see out. Saskia looked so downcast as she got out of the taxi and walked up to the front entrance.

'She's here,' I told Rosa.

The door to the contact room was open so we heard Zoe greeting Saskia.

'What happened at court?' I heard her ask.

'Maggie will tell you,' Zoe told her. 'She's in there.'

As Saskia walked in the door of the contact room, her mouth gaped open when she saw Rosa sat there.

'Mum!' she gasped. 'You're not in prison!'

'No, I'm not,' Rosa smiled. 'I'm not going to prison, Saskie. The judge let me off.'

Rosa stood up and Saskia threw herself into her arms. They were both crying now.

'I'm so happy,' wept Saskia. 'I didn't think this was going to happen. I was so sure you wouldn't be here.'

'Me too,' smiled Rosa. 'But the judge listened to us, and she knew the horrible things your dad had done to you. It was because of you that she didn't send me to prison.'

Rosa explained to her that she'd got a six-month sentence suspended for twelve months.

'But what does that mean?' asked Saskia, confused.

'It means that if I stay out of trouble and don't get convicted of any other crimes for a year then I won't go to prison,' she smiled.

I could see Saskia was in as much disbelief as Rosa. They hugged again.

I couldn't wipe the smile off my face. It was wonderful to see them both so happy and relieved.

Rosa turned to Zoe. 'I know it's probably going to take weeks but please could you organise a meeting?' she asked her. 'I want to ask for permission for Saskia to come and live with me.'

'I'm afraid that's not going to happen,' Zoe told Rosa.

'What do you mean?' she sighed.

'We don't need a meeting to do that,' said Zoe. 'I'm happy to confirm that Social Service's involvement has now ended.'

Rosa looked shocked.

'W–what do you mean?' she stuttered.

'Rosa, your parenting was never in question – we just had to wait for the court process to be resolved,' Zoe told her. 'But as you haven't been given a custodial sentence, we're happy for Saskia to come and live with you permanently.'

'Don't I have to go to court or something or have one of those reviews?' she asked.

'No,' smiled Zoe. 'No more meetings. I'm telling you that if Saskia wants to be with you, then she can return to your care full time.'

'Mum, I do, I do!' laughed Saskia, putting her arms around her mum again.

I could see Rosa was struggling to get her head around it all.

'But what do you think, Maggie?' she asked me.

'I think that I'm really happy for you two to be together again,' I smiled. 'I know that's what Saskia has wanted from the very beginning.'

However, there were a few practicalities that needed to be considered first.

'When can I go to Mum's?' asked Saskia. 'Can I move tonight?'

'I'm still in temporary accommodation, sweetheart,' Rosa told her. 'It's not very nice. It's no place for a child.'

'But I don't mind,' Saskia told her.

'I honestly wouldn't want to take you there,' replied Rosa. 'Give me a few weeks to get sorted.'

'Weeks?' Saskia sighed. 'Why do I have to have to wait that long?'

'You're happy and safe at Maggie's – it won't hurt you to stay a bit longer while I get things organised for us,' Rosa told her.

'That sounds like a good idea,' I nodded.

I knew that money was tight as Rosa hadn't been able to get a job due to her impending court case, so they would have to apply for a council property.

'There's lots we can do to help,' Zoe told her. 'Social Services can write to the housing department and they can hopefully put you on the priority list.'

But I knew that even if that happened, it could still take months rather than weeks for a property to become available.

'You're welcome to stay with me for as long as you want while your mum sorts everything out,' I told Saskia.

Zoe explained that there would be no more contact sessions at the centre.

'You're free to see each other whenever you want,' she told them. 'Maggie, are you OK for Rosa to contact you directly when she wants to see Saskia?'

'Absolutely,' I nodded.

'You can go out and do things together after school or at the weekend,' I suggested. 'And, Rosa, you're welcome at my house whenever you want.'

'So there are no more restrictions?' asked Rosa.

'Not now that all criminal proceedings are over,' confirmed Zoe.

But I could see Saskia was bitterly disappointed not to be able to go and live with her mum right away. She became very tearful as we left the contact centre.

'I'll see you soon, darling,' Rosa told her, stroking her hair.

'I love you, Mum,' said Saskia sadly.

'And I love you too,' replied Rosa.

I was so happy for them both and I knew the next few weeks were going to be filled with a lot of change. At half term, the fees ran out for Saskia's private school, so she was going to have to change school. But now that she and her mother had each other, I was confident it was going to be OK.

As the weeks went on, Rosa and Saskia enjoyed spending time together without any restrictions. Rosa was very conscious of spending too much time at my house but I was happy for her to come to me and see Saskia, rather than take her to her cramped room at the temporary accommodation.

Despite the letter from Social Services to the council, there had still been no news about a suitable flat or house.

One Saturday, they came back to mine after they'd been for a walk in the local park. They both walked in with big smiles on their faces.

'What have you two been plotting?' I teased.

'Maggie, me and Mum have got some news,' Saskia told me. 'We've decided we're going to go and live in Spain!'

'Wow,' I gasped, surprised. 'Really?'

'Yep, we decided today,' Saskia grinned.

'I just thought, why are we waiting around here for housing when we could be over there?' said Rosa. 'I have friends that we could stay with until I find a job and get back on our feet.'

I knew Spain held happy memories for them both and Rosa had a Spanish passport. I could see how excited Saskia was, but I didn't want them to get ahead of themselves.

When Saskia went to the loo, I had a quick chat with Rosa.

'I know it's sudden and a big change but it's a special place for both of us,' said Rosa. 'I know Saskia feels safe there too.'

'It sounds lovely,' I told her. 'But you'll need to check with the Probation Service that the terms of your suspended sentence allow you to go and live in another country.'

'I already have,' she nodded. 'I did that before I mentioned it to Saskia as I didn't want to get her hopes up. And I ran it past Zoe, too, just in case Social Services had any objections.'

'It sounds like you've thought of everything,' I smiled. 'I'm really happy for you. When are you thinking of going?'

'As soon as possible,' she said. 'There's nothing to keep us here.'

It was all very sudden, but I was delighted for them. I knew Saskia was impatient for them to be together.

That night, before bed, I had a quick chat with her.

'How are you feeling about going to Spain?' I asked her.

'I'm excited,' she grinned. 'I really liked it there and we won't have to move around this time. I don't think I'll think about Dad as much there as it feels like a long way away from him.'

'It's a big change,' I said.

'I'll miss my friends,' Saskia told me. 'And you. But I just want to be with my mum.'

'I know you do, flower,' I soothed. 'And I'm so pleased for you both.'

I'd grown so fond of Saskia and my happiness was tinged with sadness that she wouldn't be part of my life any more, but there couldn't have been a better conclusion for her.

I looked around the table at all the happy faces tucking into pizza. There was Vicky and her foster child, Paige, who was sat giggling alongside Edie. Then there was Louisa and Charlie chatting to Rosa, and then me and Saskia.

'I like my cake,' smiled Saskia.

Louisa and Edie had made her a chocolate cake with 'good luck' written on the top in icing.

It was a month later and the following day, Rosa and Saskia were setting off for Spain. My goodbye gift to them had been two new suitcases. They didn't have many things to take but I knew they would accumulate more stuff as they started their new life together over there.

After the meal, Saskia hugged everyone goodbye. Then it was just me, her and Rosa left.

'Goodnight, sweetheart, I'll see you bright and early in the morning,' Rosa told her.

'Mum, this is the last time we'll have to say goodbye,' Saskia said. 'We'll be sleeping in the same place again from tomorrow.'

'So we will,' grinned Rosa.

'I can't wait,' she said, giving her a kiss on the cheek.

'See you in the morning, Maggie,' she told me. 'And thanks again for everything.'

We headed back into my house. Saskia's suitcase was already packed and ready by the door. She just had a few things left to pack into her rucksack.

'You'd better get to bed now as we've got an early start,' I told her. 'Night, lovey.'

I was giving them both a lift to the airport.

'I can't believe it's my last night with you,' sighed Saskia. 'I feel a little bit sad.'

'That won't last for long,' I smiled. 'You've got such an adventure ahead of you in Spain.'

'I'm happy about going to Spain but sometimes I still feel really sad about what happened,' Saskia sighed.

'I know,' I told her. 'And that's normal. Your feelings won't change just because you're somewhere different.'

'That's what Pippa said,' she nodded, and I knew she'd been upset to say goodbye to her counsellor too.

'It's going to be fine,' I smiled. 'And I'm very jealous that you're going to be in the sunshine in Spain.'

'You can come and visit?' suggested Saskia. 'You can come and stay with me and Mum at our new flat.'

'That sounds lovely,' I told her.

But in my heart, I knew that probably wouldn't happen. Saskia and Rosa needed to move forward, and I was a reminder of everything that they'd been through. They needed to try to put the last few months behind them, and that included me.

Saskia had to live with the fact that she'd never really know the full truth about what her dad had done to her. But I was sure that, with each other's love and support, they could move forward together.

Acknowledgements

Thank you to my children, Tess, Pete and Sam, who are such a big part of my fostering today. However I had not met you when PJ and Saskia came into my home. To my wide circle of fostering friends – you know who you are! Your support and your laughter are valued. To my friend Andrew B for your continued encouragement and care. Thanks also to Heather Bishop who spent many hours listening and enabled this story to be told, my literary agent Rowan Lawton and to Anna Valentine, Vicky Eribo and Beth Eynon at Seven Dials for giving me the opportunity to share these stories.

Photo credit: Simon Way

Maggie Hartley has fostered more than 300 children while being a foster carer for over twenty years. Taking on the children other carers often can't cope with, Maggie helps children that are deemed 'unadoptable' because of their behaviour or the extreme trauma that they've been through.

She's looked after refugees, supported children through sexual abuse and violence court cases, cared for teenagers on remand and taught young mums how to parent their newborn babies.

You can find her on Facebook at MaggieHartleyAuthor, where she would love to hear from you.

When newborn baby Felix is found abandoned at a train station, the police launch a desperate search for his mum. It doesn't take long for their inquiries to lead them to Emily.

While baby Felix is placed in Maggie's care, the police and Social Services try and work out why Emily, a single mum who has gone through fertility treatment to get pregnant, has suddenly resorted to abandoning her much longed-for child.

But it's only when Maggie wins her trust that Emily reveals the extent of her secret.

Can Maggie help a desperate mother and her baby reunite?

Read on for an extract from *Please Help My Mummy*, available now in paperback, ebook and audio

PROLOGUE

The Bag on the Platform

Melissa wearily walked up the platform to her usual spot at the top end. She did this journey at 6.50 a.m. every day, so she knew exactly where to stand so the doors of the first carriage opened right in front of her and she had the best chance of getting a seat on the train.

Melissa was a nurse on a geriatric ward so she cherished the relative peace and quiet of her twenty-minute commute before she walked through the doors of the busy hospital, knowing it would be at least another twelve hours before she could walk back out of them again.

She was still lost in her thoughts as she walked to the end of the platform, her eyes half closed as the warmth of the spring sun shone on her face.

She could only see one other person waiting there – a woman with long dark hair sitting on one of the seats. But as Melissa walked towards her, the woman suddenly jumped up and brushed past her. Head down, she almost broke into a jog as she dashed back along the platform towards the station entrance.

That's a bit odd, Melissa thought to herself. Maybe the woman had decided she didn't want to catch the train after all? It was a thought Melissa was quite envious of. Part of her wished she could head home and have a leisurely breakfast with her husband Dave, and nine-year-old daughter Kayleigh, instead of creeping out the door while they were both still asleep.

Melissa walked towards the row of seats where the woman had been sitting as she wanted to get her book out. But as she put her rucksack down on one of the seats, she noticed a large holdall on the floor.

She'd left her bag.

Melissa quickly spun around but as she looked down the platform, she could see the woman had gone.

She sighed. She'd have to take the forgotten holdall to the ticket office at the front of the station and would probably miss her train. But her conscience wouldn't let her leave the bag there. What if someone less honest than herself stumbled across it and took it?

But, before she could start to reach towards the large bag, Melissa froze.

There was something moving.

Then she heard a noise that chilled her to the bone.

A loud cry.

It was the sort of distinctive wail that only came from one thing.

As she looked inside the unzipped bag, she couldn't believe what she was seeing. It was a newborn baby.

'What the hell?' she gasped.

The baby was tiny; Melissa guessed it was no more than a few weeks old. It was dressed in a yellow knitted cardigan and had a hat and little mittens on. It was wrapped in a blue woollen blanket, and pinned to it was a handwritten note. The writing was small and neat.

My name is Felix Oliver. Please look after me.

Still not quite believing what she was seeing, Melissa bent down and carefully lifted the baby boy out of the bag and into her arms.

'There, there,' she shushed, wrapping the blanket around him to protect him from the cold. 'You're OK.'

The baby looked up at Melissa with big blue eyes. He was absolutely perfect, and looked clean and well-cared-for. There was a sheepskin blanket in the base of the bag and a fluffy white rabbit; someone had obviously wanted to make sure that he was as warm as possible.

Maybe that's what the woman had been doing – waiting until someone had come along so she was sure that the baby would be found and not out in the cold on his own for too long?

What on earth possessed someone to leave a newborn at a train station? Melissa hadn't paid much attention to the woman as she had been walking quickly with her head down. But she knew, from what little she'd seen, that she wasn't a teenager or a young girl. She was definitely a woman, a well-dressed one at that.

The baby let out another cry and squirmed in Melissa's arms.

'It's OK, Felix,' she soothed. 'Don't worry, we're going to find your mummy.'

She set off down the platform to get the station staff to call the police and find out who the baby belonged to – and why on earth he'd been abandoned.